PLAN AHEAD:
Protect Your Estate and Investments

Frank J. Eberhart

Self-Counsel Press Inc.
(a subsidiary of)
International Self-Counsel Press Ltd.

Copyright © 2003 by Self-Counsel Press Inc.

All rights reserved.

No part of this book may be reproduced or transmitted in any form by any means — graphic, electronic, or mechanical — without permission in writing from the publisher, except by a reviewer who may quote brief passages in a review.

Printed in Canada.

First edition: 2003

Canadian Cataloguing in Publication Data

Eberhart, Frank
    Plan ahead: protect your estate and investments/Frank Eberhart.

Self-Counsel business series

ISBN 1-55180-405-0

1. Estate planning — United States. I. Title. II. Series.
KF750.E23 2003 346.7305'2 C2002-911520-5

Self-Counsel Press
(a subsidiary of)
International Self-Counsel Press Ltd.

1704 N. State Street   1481 Charlotte Road
Bellingham, WA 98225   North Vancouver, BC V7J 1H1
USA   Canada

CONTENTS

NOTICE TO READERS	ix
PREFACE	xi
INTRODUCTION	xiii
1 ORGANIZING YOUR PERSONAL INFORMATION	1
2 SETTING UP YOUR BUDGET	9
3 WHAT HAPPENS TO YOUR ASSETS WHEN YOU DIE?	17
1. Step-up in Basis	17
2. Transferring Property by Law	18
3. Transferring Property By Contract	19
3.1 Beneficiary designations	20
3.2 Transfer on death (TOD) accounts	20
4. Transferring Property by Probate	20
4.1 Costs of probate	21
4.2 Executor's duties	23
5. Wills and Incapacity	27
4 HOW THE NEW TAX LAWS AFFECT YOU	31
1. The Temporary Tax Relief Bill and the Sunset Rule	31
2. Step-up in Basis	32
3. Income Tax	33
4. Unified Credit	34
5. Federal Estate Taxes	35
5.1 Exemption from federal estate taxes	35
5.2 Tax rate	38
6. Gift Taxes	40
7. State Death Taxes	42
8. Inheritance Taxes	43
9. College Funding	44
10. Retirement Plan Contributions	44
10.1 The make-up provision	45

	10.2	Salary deferred compensation	46
11.	Roth IRAs		46
12.	Alternative Minimum Tax (AMT)		47
13.	Educational IRAs		48
14.	Child Tax Credit		48
15.	Dependent Care Credit		48
16.	Personal Exemption and Itemized Deduction Limitations		49
17.	Marriage Penalty Relief		50

5 TRUSTS 51

1.	What Trusts Can Do		51
2.	What Can Go into Trusts		52
3.	Advantages of Trusts over Wills		53
4.	Revocable and Amendable Living Trust (RLT)		53
5.	What Fees Are Payable to Set up a Trust?		55
6.	Definition of Income for Trusts		55
7.	Common Types of Trusts and Their Uses		56
	7.1	Pour-over wills and pour-over trusts	56
	7.2	Wealth replacement trust	56
	7.3	Irrevocable life insurance trust (ILIT)	57
	7.4	Crummy trusts	58
	7.5	A/B credit shelter or non-marital trust	58
	7.6	Qualified personal residence trust (QPRT)	60
	7.7	Grantor retained trust	61
	7.8	Qualified domestic trust (QDOT)	62
	7.9	Qualified terminable interest property (QTIP) trust	62
	7.10	Testamentary trusts	63
	7.11	Spendthrift trusts	63
	7.12	Special needs trust	64
	7.13	Defective grantor trusts (Irrevocable defective income trust)	64
	7.14	Disclaimer trusts	65
	7.15	Rabbi trust (deferred compensation)	65
	7.16	Offshore trusts	66

	7.17	Family limited partnerships (FLP)	67
	7.18	Total return trusts	67
	7.19	Dynasty trust	68
	7.20	2503(b) trust	68
	7.21	2503(c) trust	68
	7.22	Charitable lead trust (CLT) [IRC 170(f)(2)(b)]	69
	7.23	Charitable remainder trust (CRT) [IRS publication 526 REV December 2000]	69
	7.24	How to determine which charities qualify for deductible charitable contributions	71
	7.25	Generation skipping transfer tax trust (GSTT)	72
	7.26	Retirement plans and GSTT taxation	75
8.	Strategies for Estate Planning Using Trusts	76
9.	Taxation of Trusts	78
10.	Private Foundations	78
11.	Funding Forms	80

6 UNDERSTANDING YOUR INVESTMENTS 83

1.	How Do I Choose An Advisor?	83
2.	I Have Social Security. Why Do I Need to Invest?	84
3.	Calculating Your Risk Tolerance	85
4.	An Overview of the Stock Market	88
	4.1 Securities Investor Protection Act	89
	4.2 Investment basics	89
5.	Choosing between Commission and Fee-Based Investments	91
	5.1 Mutual funds	91
	5.2 Bonds	92
	5.3 Stocks	92
	5.4 WRAP	92
	5.5 Discretionary account management	93
6.	Stock Options	93
	6.1 Incentive stock options	96
	6.2 Non-qualified stock options or non-statutory stock options	97
	6.3 Net unrealized appreciation	98

7. Mutual Funds		99
7.1	Types of funds	100
7.2	What tax is payable on mutual funds?	101
7.3	Variable annuities	102
7.4	Capital gains	102
7.5	Undistributed long-term gains from closed-end funds	103
8. Bonds		103
8.1	Calculating bond yields	105
8.2	Bond swaps	105
8.3	Taxable versus tax-free bonds	105
8.4	Municipal bonds	107
8.5	U.S. treasury bonds	108
9. Planning for College		111
9.1	Section 529 college funding	111
9.2	Converting to a Section 529 plan	113
10. Life Insurance		114
10.1	Taxation of life insurance	115
10.2	Loans	116
10.3	Irrevocable life insurance trust	116
10.4	Term policies	116
10.5	Traditional whole life policies	117
10.6	Universal life policies	117
10.7	Variable universal life policies	117
10.8	Wealth replacement trust	118
10.9	Single premium life policies	118
10.10	Key person policies	118
10.11	Long-term care policies	119
10.12	Disability policies	119
10.13	As a retirement investment	119
11. Variable Annuities		120
11.1	Investors	120
11.2	Family protection and estate planning	120

11.3	Qualified plans	121
11.4	Current annuity owners	121
11.5	Guaranteed income (annuitization)	122
11.6	Charitable giving	122
11.7	Fixed charitable gift annuity	122
11.8	Medicaid planning	122
11.9	Don't annuities cost too much?	123
11.10	What happens when the owner of the annuity dies?	123
11.11	How are annuities taxed?	124
11.12	Indefinite deferral of income	125
11.13	Gift or sale of an annuity	126
11.14	Annuitization of an annuity	126
12. Mutual Funds versus Annuities		127

7 LOOKING AFTER YOUR HEALTH — 129

1. What Is the Difference between Medicare and Medicaid? — 129
2. Medicaid — 130
    - 2.1 Countable assets — 130
    - 2.2 Spend-down of assets — 131
    - 2.3 Look-back provisions — 131
    - 2.4 Fair market exchanges — 131
3. Long-Term Health Care Policies — 132
    - 3.1 Tax deductions — 134

GLOSSARY — 135

TABLES

Table 1:	Probate fees	22
Table 2:	Income tax rates for 2001 and beyond	34
Table 3:	The rules of giving	34
Table 4:	Federal estate taxes from 2002 to 2010	36
Table 5:	Federal estate taxes for 2001 and 2011	37
Table 6:	Estate and gift tax unified credit (Original table before Temporary Tax Relief Bill)	38
Table 7:	Gift taxes	40

Table 8:	State death taxes	43
Table 9:	Retirement plan contribution limits	45
Table 10:	Comparison of trusts and wills	54
Table 11:	How a wealth replacement trust works	57
Table 12:	A/B credit shelter trust for 2002 for $2 million or less	59
Table 13:	A/B credit shelter trust for 2002 for $3 million	60
Table 14:	Charitable remainder trust gifting: Cash flow projections from unitrust	72
Table 15:	Tax on trust income	78
Table 16:	Taxable equivalent yield (2002)	106
Table 17:	Section 529 state current contribution maximums	112
Table 18:	How much life insurance do I need?	115
Table 19:	Comparison of mutual funds and annuities	127
Table 20:	Social security benefits	132

WORKSHEETS

Worksheet 1:	Your personal information	2
Worksheet 2:	Your budget	11
Worksheet 3:	Balance sheet	15
Worksheet 4:	Income statement	16
Worksheet 5:	Estate planning checklist	28
Worksheet 6:	Quick reference contact sheet	29
Worksheet 7:	Federal estate tax formula	39
Worksheet 8:	Federal gift tax formula	41
Worksheet 9:	Typical forms outline	81
Worksheet 10:	Calculating Risk versus Reward	85
Worksheet 11:	Tax-loss and swap	107
Worksheet 12:	Keep track of your investments	128

DIAGRAMS

Diagram 1:	The investment cycle	9
Diagram 2:	Executor's duties	24
Diagram 3:	Generation skipping strategy	74

NOTICE TO READERS

Laws are constantly changing. Every effort is made to keep this publication as current as possible. However, the author, the publisher, and the vendor of this book make no representation or warranties regarding the outcome or the use to which the information in this book is put and are not assuming any liability for any claims, losses, or damages arising out of the use of this book. The reader should not rely on the author or the publisher of this book for any professional advice. Please be sure that you have the most recent edition.

PREFACE

I started the journey to writing this book many years before becoming a financial advisor. As a personal investor, my goal was to find good advice. After embarking on an amazing journey of seminars, brokerage houses, attorneys, certified professional accountants, advisors, and banks, I was quite appalled at the different advice, expertise, and general lack of knowledge I received from many so-called professionals. I also found that my own advice and common sense served me better than most of these professionals did. So I decided to become my own expert.

The expansion of the Internet made it easy to find the information I wanted. The problem was, how did I put it all together and translate financial concepts into understandable language? It was not an easy task.

By some quirk of fate, I ended up working in the brokerage business. It was the perfect solution to obtaining all the information I needed. I talked to clients, conducted seminars, studied to become a Certified Estate Planner, and attended continuing education courses offered by mutual fund and insurance companies. I also obtained my Series 7, Series 24, Series 63, Series 65, Life, and Health Licenses.

I have read most of the books available on trusts, estate planning, and investments, and have found that they are complicated and don't provide readers with the options they need to decide if a particular investment strategy is right for them or not.

Thus my book. It starts off with helping you establish a budget — something everyone needs, whether you're just beginning to plan your estate or have been investing for some years. The book then evaluates the benefits and options of various trusts and investments so that you can be informed before talking with a financial planner or investment advisor. Finally, it takes a look at some strategies for making sure that your finances will be sufficient to cover your medical expenses should you ever have them.

This book presents you with options that make sense and that you can understand. You may wish to use it in conjunction with a qualified professional who can help you reach your financial goals. I hope I can make a difference in your journey.

Good luck.
Frank J. Eberhart

INTRODUCTION

One of most common mistakes many of us make is to start planning our estates late in life. Whether this is because we don't want to think about the inevitable — infirmity or death — or because we don't know where to start, the reality is that it is never too soon to develop an estate plan.

It's probably just as important to know what you own as it is to understand what you own.

The planning process is straightforward:

- Identify your life goals.
- Review how close you are to meeting these goals.
- Set up a plan.
- Implement your plan.
- Review your plan annually.

What needs to be in your financial plan? You'll probably want to include provisions for some or all of the following:

- Savings
- Your children's and your education
- Mortgage protection
- Income protection
- Asset protection

- Retirement
- Succession

This book helps you plan ahead to provide for yourself and your loved ones. It discusses specific estate planning tools (such as trusts and wills) and explains how investments work and are taxed — enabling you to take control and create your own financial foundation.

Oganization and preparation are essential to a financial plan. Be prepared and be informed!

The first two chapters help you develop a personal budget. By defining your normal expenses, charitable gifting plans, emergency funding, educational, and other expenses in relation to your current net income, you can develop a good foundation for your financial decisions.

If you are using an accountant, financial advisor, or attorney to help you plan, show them the information you have completed in Chapters 1 and 2, so that they can better understand your goals and needs.

Remember, if you don't have a plan, the IRS and the government have one for you. Start today to plan for your future.

1
ORGANIZING YOUR PERSONAL INFORMATION

Being organized is key to setting up a financial plan. Knowing all your important information and that of your family can help you determine what you already have and what you need to get to secure your long-term financial future. This information can also help you establish a family tree or legacy.

Fill out the worksheets in this chapter as completely and accurately as you can. They will provide the groundwork of your financial planning and budgeting. If there is any information you do not know or understand, leave it blank until you have worked through the whole book, and then come back at the end to fill in the gaps and update the information.

Remember to keep this information updated as your situation changes. You should also make photocopies of your social security numbers, birth certificates, and other important documents and put them in a safe place.

Check the Glossary for definitions of words you do not understand.

Worksheet 1: Your personal information

1. PERSONAL INFORMATION

Full Name: _____ SS#/EIN#: _____ - _____ - _____
Home Address: _____
Home Phone: _____ Work: _____ Fax: _____
E-mail: _____ E-mail work: _____
Occupation: _____ Employer: _____
Employer Address: _____
Date of Birth: _____ Citizenship: _____
Spouse: _____ SS#/EIN#: _____ - _____ - _____
Spouse Maiden Name: _____
Occupation: _____ Employer: _____
Employer Address: _____ Phone: _____ Fax: _____
Date of Birth: _____ Citizenship: _____

CHILDREN:

Name	Address	DOB	SS#	Children	Married
_____	_____	_____	_____	_____	_____
_____	_____	_____	_____	_____	_____
_____	_____	_____	_____	_____	_____
_____	_____	_____	_____	_____	_____

You should make photocopies of your social security numbers and birth certificates and put them in a safe place.

PARENTS:

Name	Address	DOB	Name changes
_____	_____	_____	_____
_____	_____	_____	_____

SS#:
Mother: _____ Father: _____

State or Country of Birth:
Mother: _____ Father: _____

Worksheet 1 — Continued

GRANDCHILDREN:

Name	Address	DOB	Parent
_____	_____	_____	_____
_____	_____	_____	_____
_____	_____	_____	_____
_____	_____	_____	_____

GREAT GRANDCHILDREN:

_____	_____	_____	_____
_____	_____	_____	_____
_____	_____	_____	_____
_____	_____	_____	_____

PRIOR MARRIAGES:

Yours: _____

Spouse's: _____

Are there any obligations to provide child support, continued life insurance, health insurance, or alimony for the benefit of prior spouse or children? [Provide details on separate sheet.]

ESTATE PLANNING DOCUMENTS

Living Will or health directive for life support?	YES _____	NO _____
Existing Will?	YES _____	NO _____
Existing Trusts?	YES _____	NO _____
Are the trusts funded?	YES _____	NO _____

2. ASSETS

Inherited Assets:

Have you filed 706, 1040, or 1041?   YES _____   NO _____

Value of inheritance $ _____

Federal Estate Taxes paid $ _____

COMMENTS: _____
_____

Organizing Your Personal Information

Worksheet 1 — Continued

CURRENT ASSETS:

	Market Value ($)	Joint/Individual Corporate, Family Limited Partnership, Trust	Location/ Account #
Primary Residence			
Investment Real Estate			
Cash			
Stocks			
Bonds			
Certificates of Deposit			
Managed Portfolios			
Stock Options			
Annuities (Variable/Fixed)			
Life Insurance Cash Value			
Business Interests			
Managed Trusts			

(e.g., family estate trusts, investment management trusts, family limited partnerships, charitable remainder trusts, contract trusts, etc.)

Automobiles			
Jewelry, Art, Antiques			
Other Assets			

Grand Total Assets: $_____

    Minus

Grand Total Liabilities (from next page, section 3: Debt) $_____

Net Worth: $_____

4 Plan Ahead: Protect Your Estate and Investments

Worksheet 1 — Continued

3. DEBT

	Balance	Loan #	Lender
Primary Residence	_____	_____	_____
Investment Real Estate	_____	_____	_____
	_____	_____	_____
Bank Loans	_____	_____	_____
	_____	_____	_____
Business Loans	_____	_____	_____
	_____	_____	_____
Credit Cards	_____	_____	_____
	_____	_____	_____
	_____	_____	_____
Automobile(s)	_____	_____	_____
	_____	_____	_____
Other	_____	_____	_____
	_____	_____	_____

4. LIFE INSURANCE

	Policy 1	*Policy 2*	*Policy 3*
Type of Insurance *(e.g., variable, term key person, long-term care, disability)*	_____	_____	_____
Owner	_____	_____	_____
Face Value	_____	_____	_____
Cash Value	_____	_____	_____
Beneficiaries	_____	_____	_____
Is insurance on a trust or transferred to new owner for estate tax purposes?	_____	_____	_____
Insurance Company	_____	_____	_____
Loans	_____	_____	_____
Other	_____	_____	_____

Organizing Your Personal Information

Worksheet 1 — Continued

5. ADMINISTRATION OF YOUR ESTATE

YOURSELF:

	Name	Address	Relationship
Executor:	_____	_____	_____
Trustee:	_____	_____	_____
Guardian:	_____	_____	_____
Power of Attorney	_____	_____	_____
Durable Power of Attorney (Health Care)	_____	_____	_____

SPOUSE:

	Name	Address	Relationship
Executor:	_____	_____	_____
Trustee:	_____	_____	_____
Guardian:	_____	_____	_____
Power of Attorney	_____	_____	_____
Durable Power of Attorney (Health Care)	_____	_____	_____

Special instructions or requests for the above-mentioned persons in the event of simultaneous deaths: _____

_____

Worksheet 1 — Continued

6. SPECIAL NEEDS & CIRCUMSTANCES

People I wish to provide for *(e.g., parents, children, grandchildren, and yourself)*

Name	Address	Relationship	DOB
_____	_____	_____	_____
_____	_____	_____	_____
_____	_____	_____	_____

SPECIAL NEEDS REQUIREMENTS *(e.g., long-term health care policies, Medicaid/Medicare plan, QTIP trusts, special needs trust)*

_____
_____
_____
_____
_____
_____

Notes:

_____
_____
_____
_____
_____
_____
_____
_____
_____
_____

2
SETTING UP YOUR BUDGET

Your investment strategies will change as your life evolves: from being single to married, to married with children; from buying a home to planning for college; from making investments to tax planning; from planning for retirement and income protection to planning for your estate and survivor protection. (See Diagram 1: The investment cycle.)

DIAGRAM 1: THE INVESTMENT CYCLE

Income protection
(Disability/life insurance, annuities)

Housing
(Mortgage insurance)

Survivor protection
(Life insurance, income)

Financial foundation

College planning
(Section 529, Trusts, IRAS)

Estate planning
(Trusts, wills, gifting)

Investments
(Stocks, bonds, life insurance, CDs)

Retirement
(401K, IRA, ROTH IRA, annuities)

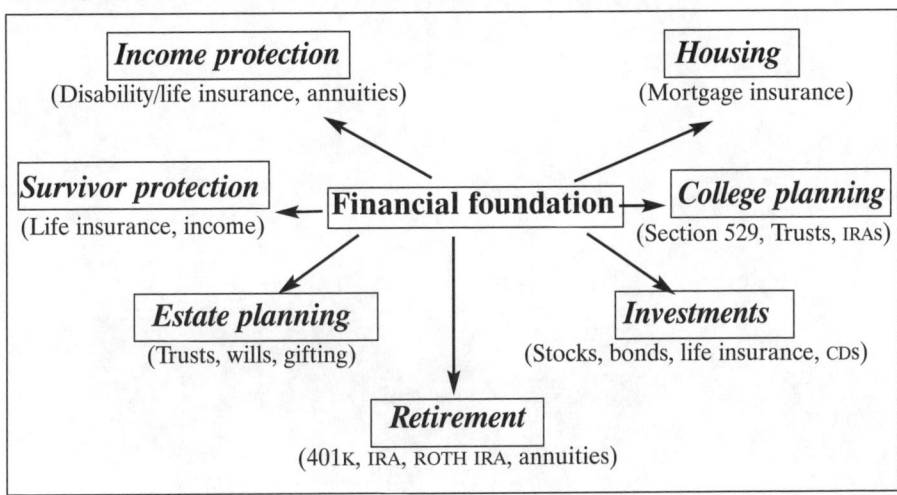

Doing your research is an essential part of the planning process, especially when choosing the people you hire to assist you to draw up your financial plan.

Make copies of the following worksheets in case you make a mistake and so that you can re-use them when you review your budget.

In each phase of your life, you need to assess where you are and where you are going. Getting organized is the first step. If you completed the personal information in Chapter 1, you've made a good start. Now you need to draw up a financial plan to help you reach your life goals. Drawing up a financial plan involves a number of steps:

a) Organizing your income and assets (drawing up a budget)

b) Determining your life goals and risk tolerances

c) Setting a time frame to accomplish your financial plan

A budget is an essential tool for establishing control of your spendable and investment income. The budget worksheet in this chapter is designed so that you can see your monthly totals as well as your annualized totals. Once you have these totals, you will transfer them to a balance sheet and an income statement. This will help you organize your assets and expenses and establish your net spendable income — as well as identify areas you need to adjust.

Regardless of how organized you think you are, let the numbers and questions contained in the following budget confirm or establish that fact. You may also wish to use the information you completed in Chapter 1 as well as this budget when consulting with your attorney or advisor about your financial goals.

Worksheet 2: Your budget

EXPENSES	Monthly	Annualized
Mortgage or rent		
Mortgage/rent	_____	_____
Property 2	_____	_____
Property 3	_____	_____
Homeowner's insurance	_____	_____
Other: (e.g., flood insurance, umbrella policy)	_____	_____
Total:	*A* _____	_____
Real estate taxes		
Property 1	_____	_____
Property 2	_____	_____
Property 3	_____	_____
Other	_____	_____
Total:	*B* _____	_____
Utilities		
Gas and electric	_____	_____
Water and garbage	_____	_____
Telephone	_____	_____
Cable TV	_____	_____
Internet/ISP	_____	_____
Miscellaneous	_____	_____
Total:	*C* _____	_____
Insurance premiums		
Life insurance 1	_____	_____
Life insurance 2	_____	_____
Life insurance 3	_____	_____
Disability insurance	_____	_____
Medical	_____	_____

Setting up your budget

Worksheet 2 — Continued

	Monthly	Annualized
Dental		
Other: (e.g., long-term care policies)		
Total:	D _____	_____
Savings/investments		
Bank accounts		
Credit union		
Certificates of deposit		
Mutual funds		
Stocks		
Bonds		
College funds		
Life (cash value)		
Annuities		
Other		
Total:	E _____	_____
Education		
Tuition and books		
Lunch		
Child care (e.g., special needs, day care)		
Other		
Total:	F _____	_____
Transportation		
Auto payment		
Auto payment		
Gas		
Insurance		
Maintenance		
Licenses		

Worksheet 2 — Continued

	Monthly	Annualized
Registrations	_____	_____
Tolls/parking	_____	_____
Miscellaneous	_____	_____
Total:	G _____	_____
Charge accounts		
Visa/MasterCard	_____	_____
American Express	_____	_____
Discover Card	_____	_____
Other	_____	_____
Total:	H _____	_____
Loan payments		
Loan 1	_____	_____
Loan 2	_____	_____
Other	_____	_____
Total:	I _____	_____
Food		
Totals:	J _____	_____
Clothing		
Totals:	K _____	_____
Other		
Travel/vacation	_____	_____
Dining	_____	_____
Contributions	_____	_____
Dues/subscriptions	_____	_____
Charitable gifts	_____	_____
Miscellaneous	_____	_____
Total	L _____	_____
Total all expenses (Add A to L)	M _____	_____

Worksheet 2 — Continued

	Monthly	Annualized
INCOME		
Gross salary 1	_____	_____
Gross salary 2	_____	_____
Rental income	_____	_____
Dividends	_____	_____
Interest	_____	_____
Capital gains	_____	_____
Commissions	_____	_____
Bonus	_____	_____
Other	_____	_____
Total:	N _____	_____
REDUCTIONS		
Federal taxes	_____	_____
State/local taxes	_____	_____
FICA	_____	_____
Social security	_____	_____
Medicare tax	_____	_____
401K	_____	_____
Other	_____	_____
Totals:	O _____	_____

Total net income (Add N + O) _____ _____

Minus total expenses (M) _____ _____

Equals net cash available savings _____ _____

Worksheet 3: Balance sheet

Assets _____

Cash _____

Checking account _____

Savings account _____

Money market _____

Life insurance
(cash value) _____

Total cash: _____ (A)

Invested assets

Stock portfolio _____

Bonds _____

IRAs _____

401K/pension _____

Mutual funds _____

Totals investments: _____ (B)

Use assets

Residence _____

Vehicles _____

Personal property _____

Investment property _____

Total use assets: _____ (C)

Total assets: _____ (A) + (B) + (C)

Assets − Liabilities = Net worth

_____ − _____ = _____

Liabilities and net worth

Auto loans _____

Mortgage _____

Credit cards _____

Loans _____

Total liabilities _____

Setting up your budget

Worksheet 4: Income statement

Gross income
Salary _____
Investment income _____

Total income: _____

Expenses
Mortgage _____
Taxes _____
Insurance _____
Utilities _____
Medical _____
Food _____
Clothing _____
Entertainment _____
Auto payments _____
Savings and investments _____
Other _____

Total expenses: _____

Income – Expenses = Surplus/(Deficit)
_____ – _____ = _____

3
WHAT HAPPENS TO YOUR ASSETS WHEN YOU DIE?

Most people do not realize that when they die, they have choices for the transfer of their wealth. The choices you make while you are living may greatly affect your estate and your heirs. Being prepared for all the complicated things that can happen to an estate takes planning, time, and an understanding of your options as well as the Internal Revenue Service and state rules. This chapter will help you learn more about your options so that you can plan accordingly.

There are three ways that your assets can be transferred when you die:

- By law
- By contract
- By probate

Before looking at these choices in more detail, let's take a look at an important concept when transferring property at death: step-up in basis.

1. Step-up in Basis

When an asset has passed through probate or from a trust, the new value of the asset is considered the new step-up in basis (fair market value) moving forward for tax purposes for the heirs. Generally, the property (e.g., stocks, bonds, and real estate) avoids capital gains and gift taxation after passing through probate or from a trust.

The new tax laws that came into effect in 2002 affect the step-up in basis of an asset. The first $1.3 million of the carry-over basis is exempt from capital gains tax. There is an additional $3 million for spousal deduction. The balance of the asset is subject to capital gains tax, regardless of whether or not it is in a trust. See Chapter 4, How the New Tax Laws Affect You, for more information.

If property appreciates after probate, capital gains tax could be due on the sale.

A half step-up in basis is when a property passes by a testamentary trust. The property has a half step-up in basis on the half that is transferred. If the survivor wants to sell the property, capital gains tax could be due on the remaining half of the property. In the case of the primary residence, the first $250,000 per person ($500,000 joint) is exempt from capital gains tax, while the balance over the exclusion is subject to capital gains tax. (See testamentary trusts in Chapter 5 for more information.)

2. Transferring Property by Law

Each state abides by either civil or common law. In common law states, if you and your partner have been living as a couple for a certain period of time (whether or not you are married), the state recognizes that you have ownership of common interests.

In contrast, civil law states recognize private rights. Currently, Louisiana is the only U.S. state whose law is based entirely on civil law. Check with your state to see which laws are applicable in your circumstances for transferring or disposing of property.

When two people jointly own property with a right of survivorship, ownership automatically passes to the survivor when one of them dies, and the property bypasses the probate process. This is often used by couples who want the survivor to receive full ownership of the property when one of them dies. The entire amount is now taxable in the surviving spouse's estate, and that spouse loses the ability to apply the unified credit.

The opposite of joint ownership with a right of survivorship is tenancy in common, where each share of ownership passes in accordance with each co-owner's individual will. (See below, **Transferring property by probate**, for more information.)

There are a few disadvantages to owning property jointly with a right of survivorship:

- If you want to sell your portion of the property, you must get the other co-owner's approval.
- You may become accountable for your co-owner's liabilities.
- If you die first, you have no way of controlling your assets. Because jointly owned assets are not controlled by your will, they transfer immediately to the surviving owner, who can dispose of the asset any way he or she wishes.
- Taking names off titles is difficult; adding co-owners is simple and an easy way to end up in court or with gift-tax violations. If your co-owner becomes incapacitated, your new co-owner may well end up being the court.

In addition, it can cause some serious problems for your heirs and beneficiaries:

- Your estate may incur a gift tax on the portion of the property gifted.
- The entire estate becomes taxable in the surviving owner's estate.
- If the survivor sells the property (includes all assets, stocks, bonds, mutual funds, and certificates of deposits), half of the sale will be subject to capital gains tax.

> **Use Worksheet 5, Estate planning checklist, at the end of this chapter, to make sure you have considered all your estate planning options.**

3. Transferring Property By Contract

Property may be transferred by a contract, such as through a trust, annuities, or a life insurance policy. With the exception of testamentary trusts, contracts that name a beneficiary bypass the probate process and are generally not subject to gift tax or capital gains tax. (Life insurance is free of income tax and estate tax if inside a life insurance trust.)

3.1 Beneficiary designations

Life insurance, annuities, IRAs, and 401K plans are examples of contracts that name a beneficiary and bypass probate. Beware, though, of some problems that can happen if you haven't done the proper planning. If you and your beneficiary named in the contract die simultaneously and you have listed your estate as beneficiary, the asset will go through probate and then be distributed to your heirs.

If the beneficiary named in the contract is incapacitated at the time of your death, the insurance or contract companies may want the courts to oversee the supervision of the assets. This is called a living probate.

3.2 Transfer on death (TOD) accounts

A transfer on death (TOD) or payable on death account is a brokerage account agreement between you and a bank or brokerage firm. By contractual agreement, upon your death, the bank or brokerage transfers assets to your beneficiaries, and you avoid probate on those assets.

TOD accounts are useful if you want to transfer an asset directly to a specified person. To avoid disputes, most accounts require a Class B beneficiary (e.g., cousin, aunt, or nephew) to file an inheritance claim form or waiver for any amounts over $25,000. Assets transferred from a TOD account receive a step-up in basis at death. The account has no bearing on any other outside assets.

> *Although transferring property through a contract is a relatively quick and simple process, there is often a cost involved. Check out the costs with your advisor.*

4. Transferring Property by Probate

If you have a will or testamentary trust, or you die intestate (i.e., without a will), your estate will go through the probate process.

A will is a written legal document administered and distributed through the probate process according to your instructions. A testamentary trust (also called *inter vivos*) is a trust written inside a will. The will goes to probate then comes back to the trust. See testamentary trusts in Chapter 5 for more information.

> **You should review your will and trust every three to five years.**

In the section above, Transferring Property by Law, we looked at property that was owned jointly with a right of survivorship. In contrast, the following property titling options are available to you if you wish to transfer your property through the probate process:

- *Fee simple*: One person holds all ownership rights and the entire estate passes by that person's will.
- *Tenancy in common*: A person owns property with other parties. Each share of ownership passes in accordance with each co-owner's will.
- *Tenancy by the entirety*: This is joint ownership between spouses only. Neither tenant (owner) can sell or gift his or her interest in the property without the consent of the other tenant. The amount included in the estate tax return is half the value of the property on the date of death.
- *Community property*: Any property acquired during marriage belongs to the husband and wife equally, regardless of how it is titled. Exceptions are any property owned prior to marriage or through an inheritance. Community property passes through probate.

Make sure that both you and your spouse have powers of attorney.

4.1 Costs of probate

If you have a will with a testamentary trust provision, the property receives a half step-up in basis on the death of the first partner. It receives the other half step-up in basis (fair market value) when the second partner dies. This can cause problems for funding (e.g., for the sale of the property), capital gains tax, and possible gift tax violations. Remember, the property receives the step-up at the date of death, but is taxable on future growth. Also, your estate could probate twice, once for each spouse.

Probate can be a costly and lengthy process:

- Creditors (e.g., Medicaid) have a right to the property before heirs do.
- Out-of-state property must go through a double probate process.

- Federal estate taxes come due nine months from the date of death and must be paid while the estate is still going through the probate process.
- If someone contests the will, the probate process will be delayed.

See Table 1, Probate fees, for some of the probate fees that are due.

The average probate process runs 9–24 months.

Once property has passed through probate and assets are distributed to the heirs, the entire amount of the property becomes taxable for federal estate taxes in the heir's estate.

Table 1: Probate fees

The following probate fees (payable for the state of New Jersey) should give you an idea of the amounts payable. Check <www.findlaw.com> or the *Blue Pages* under your county government to find the surrogate and deputy clerk of the court where you will be filing probate, and enquire about the fees payable there.

Fees of the surrogate and deputy clerk of the Superior Court

Probate of wills: $50.00

Copies of the probate: $3.00 per copy

Accounting

If no one contests the will, the attorney or executor can do an informal accounting. Otherwise the Superior Court will do an accounting.

Estate value	Cost for one page of accounting
$1 to $2,000	$50
$2,001 to $10,000	$70
$10,001 to $30,000	$85
$30,001 to $65,000	$100
$65,001 to $200,000	1/5 of 1% of the value of the estate
$200,000 and more	1/10 of 1% of the value of the estate, but not less than $400

$3.00 for each additional page

Table 1: Continued

Executor's and administrator's commissions

The following commissions are paid to the executor and administrator to settle the property of a trust:

For amounts received up to $200,000	5%
Plus for amounts received between $200,000 and $1,000,000	3.5%
Plus for amounts over $1,000,000	2%

So, for a $1.3 million estate, you would pay:

5% of $200,000	$10,000
3.5% of $800,000	$28,000
2% of $300,000	+ $ 6,000
	$44,000

Other fees

Fees are also due for the professional services of an accountant, appraiser, or attorney. Attorneys generally charge an hourly rate to probate the estate. These fees are subject to review by the court. In general, you shouldn't pay more in fees than about 6% of the gross estate.

4.2 Executor's duties

These are the steps your executor will go through to distribute your estate by probate, assuming you died testate (i.e., with a legal will), and no one contests your will. See Diagram 2, Executor's duties, for an overview of the process.

Diagram 2: Executor's duties

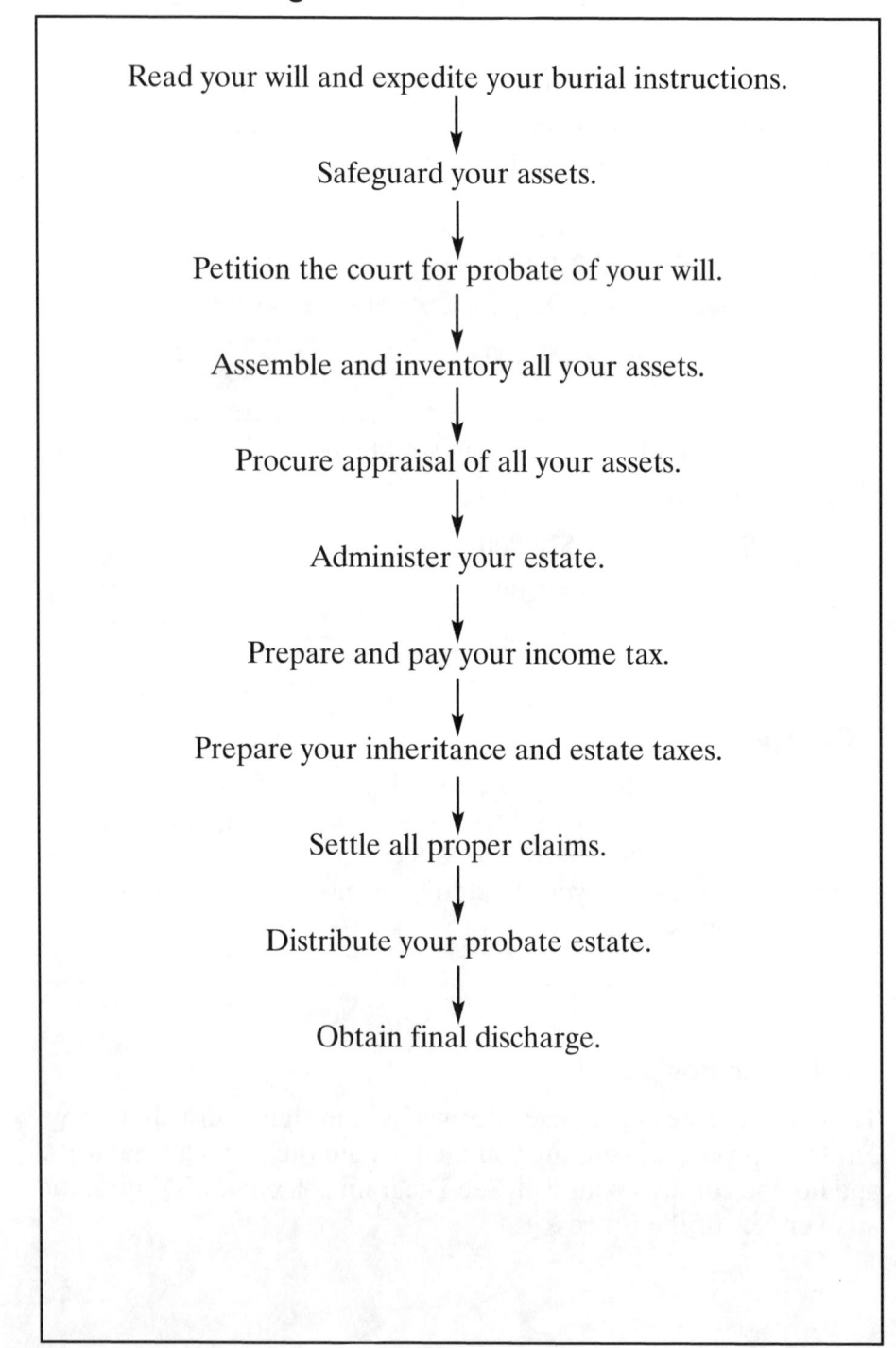

Read your will and expedite your burial instructions.
↓
Safeguard your assets.
↓
Petition the court for probate of your will.
↓
Assemble and inventory all your assets.
↓
Procure appraisal of all your assets.
↓
Administer your estate.
↓
Prepare and pay your income tax.
↓
Prepare your inheritance and estate taxes.
↓
Settle all proper claims.
↓
Distribute your probate estate.
↓
Obtain final discharge.

a) *Read your will and expedite your burial instructions:* The executor will meet members of your family and other interested parties who need aid and information. He or she confers with the attorney who drew up the will and with other people who are familiar with your financial affairs.

b) *Safeguard your assets:* The executor takes such immediate protective measures as are desirable to protect your assets. Before being appointed by the court as executor, he or she —
   - looks to the insurance and protection of real property (e.g., stocks, bonds, real estate) and personal property (e.g., jewelry, art, car)
   - secures information about your business interests
   - examines all your books and files
   - gives notice of your death to banks, safe deposit companies, and others

c) *Petition the court for probate of your will*: The executor obtains proof of heirship, locates witnesses, petitions for probate of your will and, if necessary, applies for all court orders in the administration of the estate. He or she is appointed as executor of your estate and files an oath of office.

d) *Assemble and inventory all your assets:* The executor —
   - takes proper steps to collect polices of life insurance, secures tax waivers, and collects all cash
   - inventories and appraises household goods and effects, removing valuables to a vault
   - processes all claims for amounts due, locates evidence and witnesses on contested claims
   - arranges proper supervision and management of your business interests
   - obtains custody of securities and collects all interest and dividends
   - inspects condition leases, taxes, and mortgages of real estate, and arranges for their management

e) *Procure appraisal of all your assets:* The executor gathers complete and satisfactory evidence of the value of all your assets at the date of your death.

f) *Administer your estate:* Governed by the wishes expressed in your will, the requirements of your estate, and the local probate law, the executor —
- gives special study to valuable collections and determines method and time of sale for articles not bequeathed
- makes a careful estimate of amount of cash to be raised for payment of taxes, legacies, expenses of administration, and probate net estate for distribution
- gives exhaustive study to your business interests, determines policy of continuance, liquidation, or sale with due regard to expressions in your will.
- carries out or adjusts incomplete contracts.
- makes a comprehensive review of market conditions for each security to decide which should be sold first, if necessary, to meet taxes, expenses, claims, and specific bequests
- investigates all real estate from a standpoint of earnings market and desirability in case circumstances require its sale

g) *Prepare and pay your income tax:* This is an intricate and involved procedure in which particular forms of information and returns must be filed with each taxing body. The executor —
- attends to the income tax for the part of the year before your death
- files the return and pays tax for the part of the year after your death
- makes careful survey of all possible tax claims to see that no further liability exists upon review by the government

h) *Prepare your inheritance and estate taxes:* This is an intricate and involved procedure in which particular forms of information and returns must be filed with each taxing body. The executor —
- ascertains and pays inheritance tax in your state of residence
- obtains waivers for the transfer of securities
- arranges for the necessary proceedings to release securities or property located in other states
- files the preliminary notice, prepares the return, and pays state death and inheritance tax and federal estate tax

i) *Settle all proper claims:* The executor publishes notice to creditors and obtains all available evidence regarding the propriety of each claim filed. He or she resists all improper claims and pays proper claims out of the estate funds.

j) *Distribute your probate estate:* The executor prepares a date for the final account, showing in detail all receipts and disbursements, and notifies interested persons of the hearing of the account. After the court has settled the account, the executor distributes the remaining property of your estate as directed by the court.

k) *Obtain final discharge:* After the final payment and distribution to legacies and desirees (people who have made a claim), the executor secures final discharge as executor.

The executor's job is made a lot easier if you have planned ahead and have your financial affairs in order. Once you have completed the worksheets in Chapters 1 and 2, give a copy to your executor or make sure he or she knows where to find copies in the event of your death. Remember to keep all copies up to date and accurate. You may also want to give your executor a copy of Worksheet 6, Quick reference contact sheet.

5. Wills and Incapacity

One of the most common mistakes people make when planning their estates is thinking that the executor of your estate can make decisions for you when you become incapacitated (i.e., not of sound mind or health). This is simply not true. If you are not of sound mind and you haven't prepared a living will or appointed a power of attorney, the court can step in and require guardianship.

Once the guardianship is awarded, he or she must obtain the judge's approval on all transactions for the incapacitated person (you). Any transactions must be ruled to be in your best interest, but since you are not dead, your will has no effect on your wishes.

Living will: *A document that states your wishes in reference to artificial means to keep you alive if you have a terminal injury or illness. Also called a health-care proxy.*

For more information on wills, living wills, and powers of attorney, see Wills Guide for America, *another title in the Self-Counsel series.*

Worksheet 5: Estate planning checklist

I have:

❒ Written a will and/or trust and living will that makes provisions for an executor, guardian, beneficiaries, and successor trustees

❒ Taken out a life insurance policy to cover estate taxes and living expenses for my surviving spouse

❒ Given a copy of my will and trust, together with all proper insurance policy numbers and a video to my attorney

❒ Taken out life insurance on my children to guarantee insurability

❒ Made long-term health care provisions and provided for a durable power of attorney

❒ Adequate homeowner's insurance

❒ Mortgage insurance

❒ An umbrella policy for additional liability coverage

❒ Taken out disability insurance

❒ Bought stocks, bonds, and mutual funds and put them in street name with a brokerage firm (for certificates only)

❒ An IRA or other qualified plan that names a proper beneficiary

❒ Checked into the probate rules for my out-of-state property

❒ Annuities

❒ Put copies of my and my family's social security numbers and birth certificates in a safety deposit box and given my attorney or executor the key

❒ Drawn up a business succession plan, taken out key person insurance, and drawn a buy-sell agreement to plan for who will take over my business in the event of my death

❒ Reviewed my current budget

❒ Made a filing system that identifies categories such as auto, insurance, expenses, credit cards, and investments

Worksheet 6: Quick reference contact sheet

	Family physician	Pediatrician	Eye doctor	Dentist
Name	_____	_____	_____	_____
Address	_____	_____	_____	_____
City, St., Zip	_____	_____	_____	_____
Phone	_____	_____	_____	_____
Fax	_____	_____	_____	_____
Pager	_____	_____	_____	_____
E-mail	_____	_____	_____	_____
Cell phone	_____	_____	_____	_____

	Guardians	Executor	Funeral director
Name	_____	_____	_____
Address	_____	_____	_____
City, St., Zip	_____	_____	_____
Phone	_____	_____	_____
Fax	_____	_____	_____
Pager	_____	_____	_____
E-mail	_____	_____	_____
Cell phone	_____	_____	_____

Don't forget to include a copy of your medical and prescription identification cards for each plan.

	Lawyer	Accountant	Safe deposit location
Name	_____	_____	_____
Address	_____	_____	_____
City, St., Zip	_____	_____	_____
Phone	_____	_____	_____
Fax	_____	_____	_____
Pager	_____	_____	_____
E-mail	_____	_____	_____
Cell phone	_____	_____	_____

Worksheet 6: Continued

	Financial broker	**Bank**	**Insurance agent**
Name	_____	_____	_____
Address	_____	_____	_____
City, St, Zip	_____	_____	_____
Phone	_____	_____	_____
Fax	_____	_____	_____
Pager	_____	_____	_____
E-mail	_____	_____	_____
Cell phone	_____	_____	_____

Special instructions or requests for the above-mentioned persons in the event of simultaneous deaths: _____

_____

_____

4
HOW THE NEW TAX LAWS AFFECT YOU

Knowing what taxes are due on your estate and investments can help you plan your financial future. This chapter takes a look at some of the taxes that will be levied on your estate upon your death, as well as other taxes that may affect your financial portfolio.

Consider taking advantage of some of the titling options discussed in Chapter 3 to minimize the taxes you pay.

1. The Temporary Tax Relief Bill and the Sunset Rule

In 2002, Congress enacted the Temporary Tax Relief Bill (H.R. 1836). The bill has a number of effects on estate planning, and the need for planning is perhaps even more important now than before.

The Temporary Tax Relief Bill lasts from 2002 to 2011. In 2011, two things may happen:

- The Senate may vote (by a 60% majority) to extend or reinstate the Temporary Tax Relief Bill and continue with the current rates, or
- the sunset rule will go into effect and the tax rates will return to what they were before 2002.

The likelihood of Senate voting to continue the current rates is low. The opening line of the Congressional budget prohibits the elimination of federal estate taxes due to budget restraints. Because the

Temporary Tax Relief Bill reduces and then eliminates federal estate taxes by 2010, between 2002 and 2010, the government will lose approximately $50 billion in revenue. We will also have five Congressional elections and two presidential elections during this time.

The rest of this chapter outlines the current tax laws under the Temporary Tax Relief Bill, but also refers to what may happen if the sunset rule goes into effect in 2011.

Most of the Temporary Tax Relief Bill changes went to the individual, not the corporation. The bill also affected college funding, the 401K limits, ROTH IRAs, alternative minimum tax, educational IRAs, child tax credit, dependent care credit, personal exemption limitation, and marriage relief penalty.

Under the sunset rule, all programs revert back to 2001 levels, including defined contribution plans, education, and estate taxes.

Consult your tax advisor on how or what portions of the new rules will affect you. For more information, visit the following Web sites or consult a tax professional:

- Internal Revenue Service: www.irs.gov
- 401K and defined contribution information: www.freeerisa.com
- Social Security: www.ssa.gov.com

2. Step-up in Basis

As we discussed in Chapter 3, assets receive a current market value (step-up in basis) after probate or testamentary or revocable trusts. Under present law, all transfers made at death receive a complete step-up in basis, which generally avoids capital gains tax and gift tax. The step-up applies to all trusts and after completion of probate for wills and testamentary trusts.

Under the Temporary Tax Relief Bill, in 2010 the step-up in basis will change. Each decedent will have $1.3 million exemption to transfer to a non-spouse that will receive the step-up in basis. A spouse will receive an additional $3 million of property for step-up in basis. All property (e.g., stocks, bonds, real estate) over these amounts will be carry-over basis and capital gains tax will apply. This means that while the first $1.3 million of your estate will receive no capital gains tax, the balance over this will be taxable as a long-term capital gain. You need to keep track of your cost basis. The IRS will require this (you will receive forms) for capital gains tax.

If Congress does not pass new laws or extend the current Temporary Tax Relief Bill (see the sunset rule above), the law eliminates the step-up in basis provision by imposing carry over basis rules with limited step-up allowances.

The basis is the cost of an asset at purchase date. If sold at current or fair market value, there would be a capital gain on the sale:

- If sold within the first 12 months of owning, you pay ordinary income tax at your current taxable rate.
- If sold after one year (i.e., long-term gain), you pay 20% tax.

Under current law, at death, the assets receive a step-up to basis value. This means that if you bought the stock for $200,000 and it has now appreciated to $2 million, your heirs would receive this at the new value of $2 million. If they sold the stock, they would generally not incur any capital gains tax. Note: This does not include federal estate taxes and state death taxes.

So, under the new rule, if this was a single-person exemption (i.e., no spouse) the tax would be $2 million – $1.3 million exclusion = $700,000 @ 20% capital gain (assuming it was over 12 months) = $140,000 tax due.

3. Income Tax

The income tax rate cuts under the Temporary Tax Relief Bill began in 2001 with a rebate check to all individuals who filed an income tax return and produced taxable income. The cuts will be completely phased in by 2006 and do not appear to be affected by the sunset rule.

Previously, the lowest tax rate was 15%. A new tax rate of 10% has been created. It applies to —

- the first $6,000 of taxable income for singles ($7,000 after 2007), and
- the first $12,000 for married couples filing jointly ($14,000 after 2007).

The remaining portion of the 15% rate will remain as it is under current law.

Table 2 shows the income tax rates for 2001 and beyond.

Table 2: Income tax rates for 2001 and beyond

Rate before 2001:	15%		28%	31%	36%	39.6%
Reduced to:						
2001	10%	15%	27.5%	30.5%	35.5%	39.1%
2002 – 2003	10%	15%	27%	30%	35%	38.6%
2004 – 2005	10%	15%	26%	29%	34%	37.6%
2006 – beyond	10%	15%	25%	28%	33%	35%

4. Unified Credit

The unified credit eliminates or reduces your gift tax and estate tax payable. To apply the unified credit, subtract the credit amount from any gift tax you owe. You can use the remaining unified credit against any estate taxes you owe.

The amount of unified credit you use in one year against your gift tax reduces the amount of credit you can use in future years.

The unified credit in 2001 was $675,000. So if you made a gift or had a taxable estate up to a total of $675,000, you would not pay any gift or estate tax. This amount is called the exclusion amount.

A married couple can take advantage of joint unified credits (i.e., they can combine the unified credit amount on the total estate). Under the Temporary Tax Relief Bill, the unified credit and corresponding exclusion amounts were increased from 2002 to 2009. Table 3 shows the rules of giving for gift tax purposes. See below for more information on estate taxes and gift taxes.

Table 3: The rules of giving

Year	Gift allowed each person	Lifetime exclusion amount
2000 – December 31, 2001	10,000	
2002 & beyond	11,000	1,000,000

You may gift $11,000 per calendar year to anybody without paying gift tax. If you gift more than the $11,000 per year per individual, you will pay gift tax in accordance to the highest gift tax in effect (see Table 4 and Table 5). You may apply your unified credit against your gift over $11,000, file IRS Form 709; doing so will reduce your future exclusion for estate/gift tax by the amount used. You can file an amended return using IRS Form 709 if the person(s) are still alive.

5. Federal Estate Taxes

The Internal Revenue Service knocks on the door of the estate nine months after death to collect any federal estate taxes due. If you do not have the money, the IRS can lien and levy (i.e., sell any items) to pay for the taxes due. Occasionally, the IRS grants an extension for as long as ten years. In this case, the estate will incur interest but not penalties.

The Temporary Tax Relief Bill reduces the federal estate tax through 2009. The tax is eliminated in 2010 (i.e., if you die in 2010, your estate will not be subject to estate taxes, but still subject to gift tax). In 2011, if the sunset rule comes into effect, the Temporary Tax Relief Bill expires and goes back to 2001 levels.

5.1 Exemption from federal estate taxes

Not everyone pays federal estate taxes. Your net estate must exceed a certain limit before federal estate taxes are due. This is because the unified credit is applied against your estate to reduce or eliminate the estate tax payable.

In 2001, your estate was exempt from federal estate taxes if it was under $675,000. (The unified credit was $675,000.)

Under the Temporary Tax Relief Bill, in 2002, the unified credit (exclusion amount) is $1 million per person. This amount is increasing every year to 2009, when the limit will be $3.5 million. As discussed above, in 2010, no federal estate taxes will be due if you do not exceed the exclusion amount (see Table 4 below).

For example, if your taxable estate is $1.5 million in 2002, estate tax would be due on $1.5 million less $1 million unified credit. The tax due would be 50% of $500,000 or $250,000.

If you are married, you can apply $2 million against your estate ($1 million each for you and your spouse if you establish a B trust). So, under the same scenario, a $1.5 million taxable estate would have zero federal estate tax due.

For tax purposes, your net estate includes your gross estate (e.g., life insurance, annuities, property) less your deductions (e.g., funeral expenses, debts, non-marital deduction).

The unified credit for estate taxes is calculated on IRS Form 706.

Credit shelter (B trust) can be established by wills, trusts, or testamentary trust provisions.

Table 4: Federal estate taxes from 2002 to 2010

Year	Federal unified credit	Estate/gift tax credit	Federal estate tax rate	Estimated tax*
2002	$1,000,000	$345,800	50%	$2,500,000
2003	$1,000,000		49%	$2,400,000
2004	$1,500,000	$555,800	48%	$1,920,000
2005	$1,500,000		47%	$1,880,000
2006	$2,000,000	$780,800	46%	$1,380,000
2007	$2,000,000		45%	$1,350,000
2008	$2,000,000		45%	$1,350,000
2009	$3,500,000	$1,455,800	45%	$ -0-
2010	*Taxes repealed*		*Highest gift tax rate still in effect — 35%*	
2011	$1,000,000	$1,000,000	55%	

* The tax estimates are based on a $7 million estate, using joint unified credits

If you or your spouse dies in 2010, the federal estate taxes under the Temporary Tax Relief Bill will be eliminated from your estate. The gift tax will still be in effect at a rate of 35%. Many people are confused about gifting in 2010 with the unified credit. Because there is no estate tax only if you die, you have no gifting exclusions. So you will pay 35% gift tax on any amount over the annual current gift exclusion ($11,000).

In 2011, the unified credit will revert back to $1 million if Congress does not pass new laws or extend the current Temporary Tax Relief Bill. Federal estate taxes will revert back to 55% tax, plus the 5% surtax returns on estates of $10 million but not exceeding $17.184 million.

If you did not make a gift out of your estate using your unified credit, you potentially lose $7 million in credit ($3.5 million in an A/B trust for each spouse) minus Joint unified credit of $2 million equals a $5 million loss (see Table 5 below).

Table 5: Federal estate taxes for 2001 and 2011*

Year	Value of taxable estate	Federal estate tax and gift tax
2001	$10,000–$20,000	$1,800 plus 20% of excess over $10,000
2001	20,000–40,000	$3,800 plus 22% of excess over $20,000
2001	40,000–60,000	$8,200 plus 24% of excess over $40,000
2001	60,000–80,000	$13,000 plus 26% of excess over $60,000
2001	80,000–100,000	$18,200 plus 28% of excess over $80,000
2001	100,000–150,000	$23,800 plus 30% of excess over $100,000
2001	150,000–250,000	$38,800 plus 32% of excess over $150,000
2001	250,000–500,000	$70,800 plus 34% of excess over $250,000
2001	500,000–750,000	$155,800 plus 37% of excess over $500,000
2001	750,000–1,000,000	$248,300 plus 39% of excess over $750,000
This is where 2011 will start if Congress does not reinstate the Temporary Tax Relief Bill.		
2001 and 2011	1,000,000–1,250,000	$345,800 plus 41% of excess over $1,000,000
2001 and 2011	1,250,000–1,500,000	$448,300 plus 43% of excess over $1,250,000
2001 and 2011	1,500,000–2,000,000	$555,800 plus 45% of excess over $1,500,000
2001 and 2011	2,000,000–2,500,000	$780,000 plus 49% of excess over $2,000,000
2001 and 2011	2,500,000–3,000,000	$1,025,800 plus 53% of excess over $2,500,000
2001 and 2011	3,000,000–10,000,000	$1,290,800 plus 55% of excess over $3,000,000
2001 and 2011	10,000,000–21,040,000**	$5,140,800 plus 60% of excess over $10,000,000
2001 and 2011	$21,040,000 plus	$11,764,800 plus 55% of excess over 21,040,000

*This table will be in effect in 2011 only under the sunset provision.

**In 2011, estates over $10 million have a 5% surcharge until the benefit of the unified credit and the lower graduated tax brackets have been recaptured. After $21,040,000, the tax is a flat 55%.

5.2 Tax rate

Table 4 shows the federal estate and gift taxes for 2002 to 2010 under the Temporary Tax Relief Bill, and Table 5 shows the tax rates for 2001 and 2011 (if the sunset rule takes effect). Note, however, that under the Temporary Tax Relief Bill, the tax payable is only an estimate of what the tax would be. On the old tables (i.e., 2001 and 2011) it is a flat dollar amount plus a percentage over that amount.

For example, for a $7 million net estate:

- Under the old rules, the tax payable is $1,290,800 + $2,200,000 (i.e., 55% over $3 million) = $3,490,800.

- Under the new rules, in 2002, the estimated estate tax would be $2,500,000. ($7 million net estate − $2 million exemption (using the A/B credit trust) = $5 million taxable estate @ 50% = $2.5 million tax due.

See Chapter 5 for more information on A/B credit trusts.

So the Temporary Tax Relief Bill would save your estate $990,800.

Table 6: Estate and gift tax unified credit
(Original table before Temporary Tax Relief Bill)

Year of death	Exclusion	Unified credit
1996–1997	$600,000	$192,800
1998	$625,000	$202,050
1999	$650,000	$211,300
2000–2001	$675,000	$220,550
2002–2003	$700,000	$229,800
2004	$850,000	$287,300
2005	$950,000	$326,300
2006	$1,000,000	$345,800

Use Worksheet 7 to calculate your federal estate taxes.

Worksheet 7: Federal estate tax formula

For post-1976 gifts only

A. Gross estate $ _____

B. Subtract Claims against estate _____
   (Mortgages, other debts)

   Deductions: Administration expenses _____

   Funeral expenses _____

   Marital deduction _____

   Charitable deductions _____

Total deductions: _____

C. Taxable estate: _____

D. Add: All post-1976 adjusted taxable gifts _____

E. Adjusted taxable estate: _____

F. Calculate tentative tax using the federal tax tables _____

G. Subtract: Total gift taxes paid on post-1976 _____

   Gross estate tax _____

   Unified credit _____

   *Death tax _____

   Credit for foreign death taxes _____

Totals credits: _____

H. Net estate tax _____

I. Add: Generation skipping tax transfers _____

J. Estate tax payable $ _____

*Credit for state death tax equals the lesser of a) total of such taxes actually paid or b) amount determined under the Credit for State Death Tax table. The credit for state death taxes is based on the "adjusted taxable estate." The adjusted taxable estate is equal to the taxable estate less $60,000.

6. Gift Taxes

In an effort to try avoid estate taxes, many people transfer their property, certificates of deposit, stocks, or bonds to a relative. Such gifts, however, are taxed to prevent a person from disposing of his or her property during life to avoid estate taxation. The IRS and Medicaid use the probate process to catch such processes, by checking the courthouse for 2102 property transfers, bank tapes, court filings, and probate readings.

The annual amount you are allowed to gift is $11,000 per person per calendar year. This excludes charitable gifts (see Chapter 5 for more on charitable gifts). A married couple can jointly gift $22,000 per person per year.

Gift taxes are calculated on Form 709. You can file an amended return for prior years (unless one or both persons have died).

In 2001, gifts over these limits were subject to 55% gift tax. Under the Temporary Tax Relief Bill, this percentage is decreasing, and by 2010, the gift tax rate will be 35%. See Table 7 for the current gift tax rates.

Table 7: Gift taxes

Year	Gift tax
2002	50%
2003	49%
2004	48%
2005	47%
2006	46%
2007	45%
2008	45%
2009	45%
2010	35%
2011	35%

The penalty for not paying the gift tax is severe: Penalties can range between 200% and 400% from the determined date and value of the transfer — plus the rate of gift tax in the year of the violation.

Regardless of the asset, the gift tax is evaluated and paid at the time the lifetime transfer is made. However, when the donor dies, the amount of the gift is subject to the full estate tax and a credit is given for gift taxes previously paid. The donor is responsible for the gift tax on all irrevocable gifts not sold at fair market value.

The following example shows how you can use the gift tax and unified credit to reduce the taxes due on your estate:

John Doe made a gift of $100,000 to his son in 2001. It was John Doe's first taxable gift. He filed a gift tax return (IRS Form 709), of which he subtracted the $10,000 annual exclusion (the maximum amount for 2001; in 2002 the exclusion is $11,000) and figured the gift on $90,000. He used $90,000 of the unified credit to eliminate the tax on the gift.

John Doe died in 2003. The available unified credit for 2002 was $1,000,000 (see Table 4), of which he used $90,000 and left $910,000 to apply toward the gross taxable estate filing IRS Form 706.

Lifetime transfer: *Each calendar year, you can gift $11,000 without reducing your unified credit or paying the gift tax over the annual exclusion per person. If you live to 90 years, you can do this about 90 times. The lifetime transfer would be approximately $1 million.*

Fair market value: *Items that are sold at 70% or better are considered by the IRS to be sold at fair market value.*

Use Worksheet 8 to calculate federal gift tax due.

Worksheet 8: Federal gift tax formula

For post-1976 gifts only

A. Aggregate of all prior and present gifts _____

B. Tentative gift tax on "A" (use tax table) _____

C. Aggregate of all prior taxable gifts _____

D. Tentative gift tax on "C" (use tax table) _____

E. Tentative gift tax on present gift (B less D) _____

F. Gift tax credit (2002 gift tax table) $345,800

G. Aggregate gift tax credit taken for prior post-1976 gifts
(But not more than "C") _____

H. Gift tax credit available for current gift
("F" less "G" but not more than "E") _____

I. Gift tax payable for current gift
("E" less "H") _____

7. State Death Taxes

State death taxes are levied on estates by each state for revenue generation. They may be due even if your estate is not large enough for federal estate taxes (see federal tax limits in Table 4). Under current law, the death tax is paid to the decedent's state of domicile. It is equal to the state death tax credit on the federal estate tax return.

The state death tax will be eliminated in 2005 under the Temporary Tax Relief Bill. It will be replaced with a deduction for taxes paid to any state. The National Governors' Association estimates the resulting lost revenue stream at $50 billion to $100 billion over the next ten years.

The state death tax is the same amount in every state.

Most states are imposing their own estate tax law. For example, New Jersey (and Wisconsin, following the same rules as New Jersey) passed legislation July 1, 2002 (retroactive to January 1, 2002), that uses 2000 estate tax law. New Jersey capped the exemption at $675,000 and requires a tax filing in the year of the death, taxes to be paid within nine months of the date of death, and will impose a lien against assets or property until the taxes are paid. (The exception is if all assets pass to the surviving spouse, or are in a revocable living trust, no taxes are due until the second spouse dies.)

Most states are creating their own estate tax forms for filing. These new taxes are in addition to any federal estate tax due; therefore, you could owe no federal estate taxes (both when the first and second spouse die) and still owe a substantial amount to your state of domicile.

Check with your state department of taxation, estate planning attorney, or other professional to obtain information regarding any new rules.

The phase-out period for state death taxes is as follows:
- 2002 reduces by 25%
- 2003 reduces by 50%
- 2004 reduces by 75%
- 2005 and beyond reduces by 100%

See Table 8: State death taxes

Table 8: State death taxes

Value of taxable estate	Rate of tax
$40,000 to $90,000	$0 plus 0.08% of excess over $40,000
$90,000 to $140,000	$400 plus 1.6% of excess over $90,000
$140,000 to $240,000	$1,200 plus 2.4% of excess over $140,000
$240,000 to $440,000	$3,600 plus 3.2% of excess over $240,000
$440,000 to $640,000	$10,000 plus 4.0% of excess over $440,000
$640,000 to $840,000	$18,000 plus 4.8% of excess over $640,000
$840,000 to $1,040,000	$27,600 plus 5.6% of excess over $840,000
$1,040,000 to $1,540,000	$38,800 plus 6.4% of excess over $1,040,000
$1,540,000 to $2,040,000	$70,800 plus 7.2% of excess over $1,540,000
$2,040,000 to $2,540,000	$106,800 plus 8.0% of excess over $2,040,000
$2,540,000 to $3,040,000	$146,800 plus 8.8% of excess over $2,540,000
$3,040,000 to $3,540,000	$190,800 plus 9.6% of excess over $3,040,000
$3,540,000 to $4,040,000	$238,800 plus 10.4% of excess over $3,540,000
$4,040,000 to $5,040,000	$290,800 plus 11.2% of excess over $4,040,000
$5,040,000 to $6,040,000	$402,800 plus 12.0% of excess over $5,040,000
$6,040,000 to $7,040,000	$522,800 plus 12.8% of excess over $6,040,000
$7,040,000 to $8,040,000	$650,800 plus 13.6% of excess over $7,040,000
$8,040,000 to $9,040,000	$786,800 plus 14.4% of excess over $8,040,000
$9,040,000 to $10,040,000	$930,800 plus 15.2% of excess over $9,040,000
$10,040,000 +	$1,082,000 plus 16.0% of excess over $10,040,000

The phase-in period for state estate tax started in 2002.

8. Inheritance Taxes

Some states charge an inheritance tax on estates. Inheritance taxes are (in most states) taxes due by any Class B beneficiary. Class A beneficiaries do not pay inheritance taxes. Instead, they apply the tax on any money collected by them from the estate. For example,

New Jersey charges 11% inheritance tax (up to 15% on certain beneficiaries) on non-spouse assets received from an estate. Check with your state to see if inheritance taxes apply.

9. College Funding

One of the more unfortunate victims of the Temporary Tax Relief Bill is the Section 529 plan for college funding, which was born in the Taxpayer Relief Act of 1997. In 2001, Congress allowed tax-deferred and tax-free withdrawals from Section 529 plans for educational purposes.

However, in 2011, the sunset rule will eliminate the tax-free withdrawals. Section 529 investments will still grow tax deferred as far as we know. Pressure is on Congress to keep the tax-free withdrawals if they are used for higher education.

See Chapter 6 for more information on Section 529 accounts.

10. Retirement Plan Contributions

Let's start with some definitions of retirement plans covered in this section:

- An IRA is an individual investment retirement account.
- A 401K is an employer-sponsored defined-contribution plan
- A Simple IRA is an employer-sponsored defined-contribution plan. It requires mandatory contribution matches by the employer and W2 wage reporting, and allows smaller contributions.
- A 403(b) is a tax-sheltered annuity retirement plan for certain employees of public schools, tax-exempt organizations, and certain ministers.
- A 457(b) plan is a federal government defined contribution plan.

The rules for 401K and IRA contributions have changed under the Temporary Tax Relief Bill. Starting in 2002:

- contributions by employees have increased,
- there is greater flexibility for withdrawals, rollovers, and continuation of plans, and
- employers' contributions have higher deductions.

44   Plan Ahead: Protect Your Estate and Investments

Table 9 shows the retirement plan contribution limits in effect under the Temporary Tax Relief Law. Note that all limits are indexed for inflation. All contribution limits resort back to 2001 levels if the sunset rule goes into effect:

- 401K — $10,500
- IRAs — $2,000
- Simple IRAs — $6,500

You can get the IRA minimum distribution incidental benefit at www.IRS.gov.

Table 9: Retirement plan contribution limits

	IRA IRA limits	Additional and deferred if you are over 50	401K/403(b)* 457(b) plans	Simple IRA
2001	$2,000			
2002	$3,000	$500	$11,000	$7,000
2003	$3,000	$500	$12,000	$8,000
2004	$3,000	$500	$13,000	$9,000
2005	$4,000	$500	$14,000	$10,000
2006	$4,000	$1,000	$15,000	$10,000
2007	$4,000	$1,000		
2008 – beyond	$5,000	$1,000		

* Does not include the make-up provision.

10.1 The make-up provision

If you are over 50 and have reached the maximum allowable contribution to your retirement plan, IRA, 401K, 403(b), Simple IRA, or ROTH IRA, you can contribute additional dollars based on the limits set out each year. This is called the make-up provision. The new contribution limits are being phased in from 2002 to 2006:

- 2002: $1,000 per year
- 2003: $2,000 per year
- 2004–2005: $4,000 per year
- 2006 and beyond: $5,000 per year

A note for employers: *If you are a trustee and fiduciary, the Department of Labor requires that you have an investment policy for your plan. The liability for not doing so can be up to the full value of your estate. Not only do you need the investment policy, but you must also invest by its discipline.*

How the New Tax Laws Affect You

You must meet the annual contribution limit maximum before making additional make-up contributions. Employers are not required to match the make-up provision. Employers who are capped at a low percentage of contribution for their 401K can contribute the make-up in addition to their regular contribution.

10.2 Salary deferred compensation

The Simple IRA allows employees to contribute up to 3% of their salary for a maximum of $7,000 (2002 amounts). In addition, they can add an additional $7,000 deferred compensation with payroll deduction. For example, if your salary is $100,000 per year, you can contribute $3,000 (3% of $100,000) plus an additional $7,000 for a total contribution of $10,000, based on 2002 contribution limits.

The employer does a match of whatever the employee puts in — but only on the salary, not on the deferred compensation. The salary deferred compensation for Simple IRAs increases at the same rate as the 401K and IRA contribution limits. The deferred compensation contribution is also pre-tax dollars.

If you wish to take income from IRAs or other qualified plans, but have not yet reached 59½, you may take substantially equal payments for five years (Rule 72t). This avoids the 10% penalty imposed for early withdrawal. Ordinary income tax does apply.

11. Roth IRAs

A Roth IRA is like an IRA. The difference is that you pay your taxes upfront and you cannot deduct contributions. Unlike an IRA, with a Roth IRA, qualified distributions (including growth) are tax free, and you do not have to take mandatory distributions after the age of 70½.

Effective in 2006, the Temporary Tax Relief Bill allows employers to create a new type of elective deferral program called the Qualified Roth Contribution Program. Participants contributing to 401K or 403(b) annuity programs may designate a portion of their contributions as ROTH contributions. Some specific rules apply to this new deferral program, so consult your tax advisor on how they affect you.

The new law provides faster vesting on matching contributions. Starting in 2002, an employee:

Vesting: *A schedule when all of the employer contributions or stock options granted over time become the employee's.*

Rollover provisions: *Individuals can transfer (rollover) previous 401Ks and IRAs from previous employers or consolidate several IRAs into one account. Rolling the account over avoids making it a taxable event. In order to avoid the 20% mandatory withholding, the rollovers should be made out to the broker or bank for the benefit of the individual.*

- must become fully vested after three years of service (previously it was five years), or
- must become vested in increments of 20% each year, beginning with the second year of service, with full vesting after six years of service (previously it was seven years).

The new bill also provides for rollover provisions, allowing rollovers into other types of vehicles, such as 401K, 403(b) annuities, or Section 457 plans. Previously, you had to roll into an IRA-rollover vehicle.

12. Alternative Minimum Tax (AMT)

The Tax Reform Act of 1986 initiated the alternative minimum tax (AMT). It was designed to ensure that high-income individuals and families could not avoid tax liability using exclusions, deductions, and credits. The primary purpose for AMT is the ability to tax deductions.

For more information on alternative minimum tax, see Chapter 6, Investments.

According to the Joint Committee on Taxation, once the Temporary Tax Relief Bill rate reductions are phased in, the number of taxpayers subject to AMT will increase from 1% to more than 11%.

Individuals with incentive stock options may find themselves with a large tax bill when the sales price of the shares is less than the value of the stock on the exercise date.

Taxpayers who were subject to AMT before the Temporary Tax Relief Bill will receive no rate reduction (see the section on income tax rate reduction above). AMT rates are still —

- 26% for the first $175,000 of AMT income after applying the exemption of $45,000 for joint filers and $33,750 for single filers, and
- 28% for the balance.

Qualified educational expenses include elementary and secondary education.

From 2001 to 2004, the AMT exemption will increase by —

- $4,000 for joint filers for a total of $49,000, and
- $2,000 for single filers for a total of $35,750.

In 2005, the tax exemption returns to the current AMT. Check with your accountant to see if AMT will affect you.

13. Educational IRAs

The Temporary Tax Relief Bill increases contribution limits on educational IRAs from $500 to $2,000 for 2002. It remains at this level until 2010, when it will probably go back to the old limits ($500) under the sunset provision. Taxpayers now have until April 15 of the year following the taxable year to contribute (they previously had until December 31 of the current taxable year).

Educational IRA contributions are not tax deductible, but the earnings accumulate tax free. The new bill waives contribution and distribution limitations for special needs students. You cannot claim both a deduction and a Hope Scholarship or Lifetime Learning Credit in the same year for a student's higher education expenses.

14. Child Tax Credit

Your personal exemption is line 38 times the number of dependents claiming. You must have the correct taxpayer identification numbers to qualify as a dependent. The $3,000 personal exemption was decreased and then increased for inflation in 2002.

Under the Temporary Tax Relief Bill, the child tax credit will increase over 10 years to:

- $600 from 2001 to 2004
- $700 from 2005 to 2008
- $800 in 2009
- $1,000 in 2010

The credit will phase out for singles and head of households whose income is over $75,000 ($110,000 for married couples filing jointly).

15. Dependent Care Credit

Dependent care credit is a credit you receive for the care for any child under your guardianship.

Under the Temporary Tax Relief Bill, the dependent care credit will increase for the period 2002 to 2010 —

- for one eligible dependent from $2,400 (in 2001) to $3,000, and
- for more than one eligible dependent from $4,800 (in 2001) to $6,000.

The credit percentage will increase from 30% to 35%.

Employers that provide dependent care can claim a tax credit of 25% of qualified expenses for employee child care. Qualified expenses include —

- costs to acquire construct, rehabilitate, or expand a facility for child care, and
- operational costs for the facility.

16. Personal Exemption and Itemized Deduction Limitations

Under the Economic Growth and Tax Relief Reconciliation Act of 2001, the phase-out of personal exemptions and itemized deductions (e.g., mortgages) are primarily aimed at higher income tax payers.

The deduction for personal exemptions (line 38, Form 1040) may be reduced or eliminated for higher income tax payers whose adjusted gross income (AGI, line 34, Form 1040) exceeds the following income thresholds:

- Married filing jointly/surviving spouse: $206,000
- Single: $137,300
- Head of household: $171,650
- Married filing separately: $68,500

The phase-out of the personal exemption will be:

- One-third in 2006–2007
- Two thirds in 2008–2009
- Eliminated completely in 2010

The amount is reduced by 2% for each $2,500 exceeding the thresholds, but cannot exceed 80% of the total deductions. For example, if you had $10,000 in deductions, the reduction amount cannot exceed $8,000. Reductions do not pertain to medical expenses, investment interest, casualty, or theft.

In addition, itemized deductions beginning in 2006 (schedule A, Form 1040) are reduced by 3% of the excess of the above-mentioned income thresholds.

17. Marriage Penalty Relief

Under the Temporary Tax Relief Bill, starting in 2005, the standard marriage penalty relief deduction for joint filers will increase each year until 2009, when it reaches the level of twice the amount of the single standard deduction. The 15% tax bracket for joint filers will also increase each year until 2008, when it reaches twice the standard single deduction.

5
TRUSTS

A trust is a legal entity that holds assets and property for the benefit of another person — the trust's beneficiary. A trustee administers the trust.

In this chapter we look at what can go into trusts and what they can accomplish. We take an in-depth look at each trust and its primary purpose, and some strategies for planning ahead using various trusts. Remember, trusts are not do-it-yourself items, and most states have different requirements for trusts and probate. It is best to consult with a professional to make sure the trust uses the proper terminology, has appointed the right power of attorney and right health care policy, and has a financial proxy that fits your specific need.

Make sure you have completed the information in Chapters 1 and 2 when you visit your attorney. This information will help him or her decide whether you should draw up a will or a trust.

1. What Trusts Can Do

Trusts are useful vehicles for the following:

- Ensuring the orderly and private transfer of assets
- Making a tax-advantaged charitable gift

Grantor: *A person who creates a trust or directly or indirectly makes a gratuitous transfer of property to a trust (which includes cash). If the person creates or funds a trust on behalf of another person, both persons are treated as grantors of the trust.*

Revocable trust: *A trust that allows the donor to change, revoke, or cancel the trust any time. A revocable trust is considered a grantor trust and is taxed to the grantor rather than to the trust.*

- Securing the cost of providing for an elderly relative, parent, or disabled child (special needs trust)
- Helping finance education (education trust)
- Avoiding probate costs and delays
- Protecting assets from creditors' claims (irrevocable trusts)
- Providing a structured way to administer your personal and financial affairs should you become incapacitated
- Managing the assets for the benefit of your heirs
- Giving you control over your assets
- Providing continuation of alimony, child support, and assets for children in case of divorce or death
- Avoiding capital gains tax (generally)
- Avoiding gift tax (generally)

2. What Can Go into Trusts

The follow assets can go into trusts:

- Stocks, bonds, brokerage accounts
- Real estate, both in state and out of state
- Mutual funds
- Variable annuities
- Capital management accounts
- Life insurance
- Art and collectibles
- Personal possessions

Durable power of attorney: *A document that allows an individual to make financial or health decisions for you if you become incapacitated.*

The following assets cannot go into trusts:

- *IRAs, pension plans, 401Ks, 403(b)s, and other qualified plans:* You can, however, change the beneficiary of these plans to be the trust, so that all assets come into the trust first, and are then distributed to the beneficiaries.
- *Life insurance policies:* If you leave life insurance in your name and make the trust the beneficiary, it is counted at face value in your gross federal estate for tax purposes. You need to place life insurance into an irrevocable life insurance trust (ILIT) or

transfer it to a new owner to remove it from the estate. Remember, though, if you transfer the policy to a new owner and the cash value exceeds the annual gift exclusion, you may trigger a gift tax for the amount over the credit of $11,000 three-year look-back on existing policies for estate-tax purposes.

3. Advantages of Trusts over Wills

By establishing a trust, you generally avoid probate costs and delays. Unlike a will, which is a public instrument, trusts are private. As well, a trust receives an immediate step-up in basis on its assets for the first spouse and again after the second spouse dies. This means that you do not pay capital gains or gift tax on the assets held in the trust. The new market value of the assets is calculated at the date of death. It is easier to transfer assets to the surviving spouse or beneficiaries from a trust, than with a will.

4. Revocable and Amendable Living Trust (RLT)

The revocable and amendable living trust (RLT) is a legal entity designed to hold or manage assets for an individual. The individual transferring assets to the trust is the grantor. Generally both spouses are trustees and beneficiaries. The grantor outlines the terms of the trust.

In an RLT, you are the trustee and you control your assets while you are alive, just like with a will. You can buy, sell, and trade your assets, and nothing really happens until you die. It is recommended that you file for a federal identification number (EIN) and title property, investments, and other items of value into the name of the trust (e.g., John Doe revocable living trust). You file Form 1041 and mark Grantor Trust.

Since the RLT is considered a revocable grantor trust, the tax goes to the grantor, not the trust. The IRS requires no additional tax filings for an RLT, and you do not need to file a separate tax return. Typically you can use your social security number and Form 1040 or 1041 with a Schedule A attachment to list all the assets to be assigned to the trust. At your death, the surviving trustee files for the tax identification number. If someone other than you or your spouse is the trustee of the RLT, then you must file Form 1041 (grantor trust). In this case, the tax goes to the trustee, not the trust.

Sprinkle provision: Gives the trustee discretionary authority to distribute income or principal in unequal amounts to beneficiaries.

Table 10 examines the advantages of a trust over a will.

Table 10: Comparison of trusts and wills

Trust	Will
Is established while you are alive. It offers no immediate tax savings.	Is established while you are alive. It offers no immediate tax savings.
Has no probate for out-of-state property.	Out-of-state property is probated in that state, and then comes back for probate in the home state of residence.
There is an immediate step-up in basis of all assets on the first spouse and a step-up after the second spouse dies.*	There is a half step-up in basis after probate for the first spouse, and a half step-up after probate when the second spouse dies.
Generally avoids gift tax.	Gift tax is possible after probate.
Generally avoids capital gains tax (except testamentary trust).	Capital gains tax is possible on both spouses after probate.
Allows a durable power of attorney if you become incapacitated (i.e., unable to make decisions).	The court oversees financial affairs if you are incapacitated. (A will does not provide for incapacity as you are still alive.)
Can establish an A/B credit shelter trust to take advantage of the unified credit.	Must use his/her wills and split assets to take advantage of the unified credit.
Generally, estate passes to heirs within 30 days or less.	Average probate is 9 months to 24 months.
Avoids probate costs and delays.	The estate pays for court costs, legal fees, appraisals, and executor's fees. These can be as high as 6% of the gross estate. They can be more if the will is contested. (One-third of all contested wills are tossed out.)

Trusts inside wills are referred to as testamentary trusts (inter vivos). If you die, the will is probated and then comes back to the trust.

54   Plan Ahead: Protect Your Estate and Investments

Avoids fiduciary bonds.	Fiduciary bonds are generally required to insure the assets and beneficiaries from any losses in their portfolios.
Information contained in the trust is private.	Information contained in the will is public.
Minimal court control of minor children. The trustee you selected manages the inheritance and provides funds for expenses until children reach attained age, or the age you specify. The court approves the guardian, not the inheritance.	The court controls minor children's inheritance and appoints guardian. All financial decisions need court approval. Inheritance goes to children at attained age.

Florida and California are the toughest probate states.

*Under the new Temporary Tax Relief Bill, in 2011 under the sunset rule, trusts lose their ability to take advantage of the step-up in basis on capital gains tax. The new law will allow $1.3 million and an additional $3 million exclusion for spousal deduction against capital gains tax. See Chapter 4, for more information.

5. What Fees Are Payable to Set up a Trust?

If you use a corporate organization (e.g., money manager, brokerage firm, or bank) as a successor trustee to manage the funds for your heirs and distribute income or funds according to your trust wishes, the fee is generally around 1% of assets under management plus any administration fees. Make sure you ask what the total cost would be.

The executor or executrix of the estate has a personal liability in managing assets to the trust, and any beneficiary can sue for losses in value. Make sure you explain this to your elected executor or executrix. Costs to set up wills with testamentary provisions or revocable living trusts vary from $1,000 to $3,500.

The person managing the trust assets (trustee/fiduciary) is personally liable for the growth of the portfolio. The trustee is managing the trust for the purpose of all beneficiaries.

6. Definition of Income for Trusts

Section 643(b) of the Internal Revenue Code has been revised to include a change in the definition of trust accounting income under

Trusts 55

state law. It also clarifies the treatment of capital gains distributed under net income under Section 643(a)(3). It will determine income taxation of trusts, including ordinary trusts, pooled income funds, charitable remainder trusts, trusts that qualify for the gift and estate tax marital deduction, and trusts that are exempt from generation skipping transfer taxes.

Most states have also incorporated the prudent investor standard for managing trust assets (i.e., total positive return to help maximize the returns of the trust using a mixture of equities and bonds).

7. Common Types of Trusts and Their Uses

This section looks at many common types of trusts and how they can be used to plan your estate for yourself and your beneficiaries. Check with your financial professional or tax attorney for more information relating to your circumstances.

7.1 Pour-over wills and pour-over trusts

A pour-over will pours the assets from the will into an existing trust created before the death of the testator. A pour-over will must go through probate, and any assets not placed into the trust before death will be subject to the jurisdiction of the probate court and controlled by the terms of the pour-over will.

The pour-over trust is usually revocable and is created before death. The trust is generally designed for a person's lifetime, and upon death, the trust dissolves and all the assets "pour over" to the grantor's estate to be controlled by his or her will. This also ensures the jurisdiction of the probate court.

7.2 Wealth replacement trust

A wealth replacement trust (WRT) is a life insurance policy held in trust. The trust removes the incidence of ownership from the grantor, thus removing the policy from the taxable estate. The life insurance policy provides money to your heirs or beneficiaries. The money is income tax and estate tax free, and is normally distributed as a lump sum to heirs. If you prefer to have more options and control over the distribution of your assets, look into a qualified terminable interest property (QTIP) or family trust.

> **Incidence of ownership:** If life insurance policies have incidence of ownership, it means that you have the ability to change beneficiaries, and write checks and withdraw cash from a policy. However, if you do any of these things, the IRS will bring the policy back into your estate for tax purposes.

Remember, any life insurance policy that is in your name is income tax free to the beneficiaries. It is calculated at the face value of the policy in your estate, unless it is placed into a trust or you are not the owner. Existing life insurance has a three-year look-back provision for estate tax purposes. New policies are estate tax free (as of the date that the policy was issued).

Table 11 shows how a wealth replacement trust works.

Table 11: How a wealth replacement trust works

Second-to-die policy value (face value life insurance policy)	$1,000,000
*Annual premium based on 47 year-old male, non-smoking, preferred risk)	$17,000
Proceeds of life insurance to heirs	$1,000,000
Tax on life insurance	$ 0
Net proceeds	$1,000,000
Net to heirs (estate & income tax free)	$1,000,000 (now taxable in the beneficiaries estate)

*For illustration only. Actual tax and life insurance will vary according to new tax laws, health risks, and other tax obligations.

7.3 Irrevocable life insurance trust (ILIT)

Life insurance counts at face value of your taxable estate for federal estate tax purposes. It is only income tax free if it is not in a trust. Irrevocable life insurance trusts (ILIT) remove the incidence of ownership of life insurance policies from your estate.

The trust owns the policies and upon death, provides the necessary funds to pay for estate taxes, death taxes, and final expenses. It distributes the proceeds of the life insurance policy income tax free and estate tax free to whomever you designate. The use of crummy powers to pay premiums makes it a gift of present value to qualify for the gift tax exclusion. The money can be placed into trust for management on behalf of the heirs as previously set up under the trust instrument, or in lump sum distribution. The money is now taxable in the heirs' estates.

Look-back provision: *The IRS has the power to bring a policy back into a taxable estate. For existing policies, they can go back three years under a will, or five years under trusts. New policies do not have a look-back provision.*

Crummy powers: *The placement of the power of appointment into a trust. This allows additions to the trust to qualify for the annual gift exclusion. The trust beneficiaries have the right to withdraw trust assets up to the annual exclusion. (See later in this chapter for more on crummy powers.)*

Gift exclusion: *The annual amount allowed per individual to gift to another individual in each calendar year. It is currently $11,000 per person, and $22,000 joint. It is commonly used to fund generation skipping transfer tax trusts, legacy trusts, and life insurance trusts. See Chapter 4 for more details.*

Existing life insurance policies that are placed into an ILIT have a three-year look-back provision for estate taxes. Your annual gift exclusion is reduced by the amount of the premium. New policies are estate tax free immediately and do not affect your annual gift exclusion for premium payment.

There are two types of ILITs:

- *Funded ILIT:* A funded ILIT consists of non-insurance assets as well as life insurance policies. The income from the non-insurance assets provides funds to pay premiums on the policy in the trust. The grantor must report the trust income generated as annual income.
- *Unfunded ILIT:* An unfunded ILIT consists only of life insurance policies. The trustee relies on crummy powers to allow the donor to declare annual gift exclusions made to the trust to pay premiums.

7.4 Crummy trusts

A crummy trust means that the power of appointment is placed into the trust. It is generally used to fund irrevocable life insurance trusts. A separate account is usually established for the trust (in the case of married individuals), and each person writes a check to the separate account on behalf of the other. The separate account then pays the premium to the trust.

Second-to-die policy: *A life insurance policy where nothing happens to the policy when the first spouse dies. When the second spouse dies, the money is distributed according to the wishes of his or her will or trust.*

Beneficiaries have the right to remove surplus funds (up to the amount of the annual gift exclusion) from the life insurance cash values. If they do, however, it could cancel the trust powers and bring it back into the estate for tax purposes. This is to avoid incidence of ownership. The crummy trust allows additions to the trust to qualify for the annual gift tax exclusion of each person or beneficiary named.

Common uses of the crummy trust are for funding life insurance policies, generation skipping tax trusts, and 2503(b) income trusts.

7.5 A/B credit shelter or non-marital trust

An A/B credit shelter trust (also called a living trust, disclaimer trust, or non-marital trust) is designed for federal estate tax purposes only. It provides income for the surviving spouse. Generally it is funded at death when the "B" trust becomes irrevocable up to the unified credit amount. You file Form 706 to activate your credit and the trust.

Most people do not fund (i.e., put in money or property) the "B" trust until death. If the "B" trust is funded now (keep tax efficiency in mind since it will be taxed at trust rates), it will remain estate tax free regardless of growth for as long as the trust remains in force.

Table 12 shows an A/B credit shelter trust for 2002 for an amount of $2 million or less.

Don't confuse the unlimited marital deduction with the unified credit. Most states allow assets to pass to the surviving spouse without paying estate taxes. However, the full amount is now taxable in the surviving spouse's estate.

Table 12: A/B credit shelter trust for 2002 for $2 million or less

TRUST A (Surviving spouse)		TRUST B (Deceased spouse)	
Half of common trust	$1,000,000	Half of common trust	$1,000,000
2002 exemption	-1,000,000	2002 exemption	-1,000,000
Taxable estate	$0	Taxable estate	$0
BENEFICIARIES		**BENEFICIARIES**	
		The B trust is to provide for the surviving spouse if established with a revocable trust assets receive full basis-step-up	
$1,000,000		$1,000,000	
Estate is tax free		Estate is tax free	
No probate if trust is established while alive		No probate if trust is established while alive	
Probate possible if trust is established by a will (testamentary)		Probate possible if trust is established by a will (testamentary)	

Trusts

Table 13 shows an A/B credit shelter trust for 2002 for an amount of $3 million (category of $2.1 million or more).

Table 13: A/B credit shelter trust for 2002 for $3 million

TRUST A (Surviving spouse)		TRUST B (Deceased spouse)	
Balance of estate	$2,000,000	Placed in irrevocable non-marital trust	$1,000,000
2002 exemption	-1,000,000	2002 exemption	-1,000,000
Taxable estate	$1,000,000	Taxable estate	$0
Approximate estate tax due @ 50% under the Temporary Tax Relief Bill	$500,000		

7.6 Qualified personal residence trust (QPRT)

A qualified personal residence trust (QPRT) is an irrevocable trust that uses gift tax or unified credit to offset the tax burden to the heirs of a personal property. It is used to keep a family or vacation home out of your estate.

The grantor of the QPRT places his or her principal personal (or vacation) residence into the irrevocable trust and he or she retains the right to live in and use the residence for a fixed term of years. The grantor pays gift tax based on the value of the transferred property, discounted by the value of the retained interest. You can also apply the unified credit using a discounted value based on the same terms as the gift tax. (See Chapter 4, How the New Tax Laws Affect You, for more information on the unified credit.)

During this term, the grantor pays taxes and mortgages and treats the property as his or her own. At the end of the term, the trust terminates and the residence passes to the beneficiaries as specified in the trust, or it may continue in trust for the beneficiary's benefit. If the grantor exceeds the term of the contract, the IRS states that he or she must rent at fair market value, and the beneficiaries of the property must pay income tax on the rent payments. The rent payments still remove dollars from the estate and the money still goes to the designated beneficiary.

If the grantor survives beyond the term, he or she will have transferred the value of the property (plus appreciation) out of the taxable estate. If the grantor does not survive beyond the term, the property goes to the beneficiaries but it will be included in the taxable estate. You may also elect to transfer the remainder interest to a charity with the same arrangements to pay taxes, insurance, maintenance, and upkeep.

The gift tax valuation is based on the value of the property, the grantor's age, the term of the QPRT, and the current federal interest rate. The property can be used as a business under certain conditions. The QPRT also allows for a certain amount of cash if held in a separate account for expenses. You can sell the primary residence if you reinvest the entire proceeds into a new residence within two years. The trust may allow insurance on the residence.

Note: If you use a limited liability company to place your primary residence in for liability protection, you lose the $500,000 capital gain exemption on the sale of the property, and it does not exempt the property from federal estate taxes.

7.7 Grantor retained trust

Also called grantor retained annuity trusts, grantor retained income trusts, and grantor retained unitrusts. The grantor retains the use of income from property for a certain number of years. Provided the grantor outlives the term, the assets can be given away at a discounted value. The value is the value of the assets at the time of the gift less the value of their interest retained. If you held assets until death, they would receive a step-up in basis for the purpose of a sale (i.e., no capital gains tax). However, the assets are taxable in your estate for federal estate taxes. If the grantor does not survive the term, the assets are taxed in the grantor's estate.

Limited liability company (LLC): An entity formed under state law by filing articles of organization as a limited liability company. None of the members of the LLC are personally liable for its debt. One of the primary uses for LLCs is to shelter rental properties. If each property has its own LLC, any entity that sues for damages or injury would have to sue each LLC. This means that the liability is limited to that property, not all properties — and not to the individual.

Unitrust: *A unitrust pays income to a beneficiary as a fixed annual percentage of the trust assets' value. The percentage remains the same for the entire term of the trust agreement.*

Annuity trust: *An annuity trust pays a fixed annual amount to a beneficiary for the term of the trust agreement.*

7.8 Qualified domestic trust (QDOT)

A qualified domestic trust is a trust designed specifically for non-U.S. resident spouses. The trustee spouse must be a U.S. citizen to qualify. (Check the Treaty Agreement to see which exclusions apply.) The surviving spouse receives income from the trust, but for estate tax purposes the IRS does not want the money to leave the country before the death of the second spouse.

QDOT trusts must have an EIN (taxpayer identification number) to qualify. Marital and charitable deductions are allowed if they are inside the QDOT on the date of death or if the surviving spouse had previously been a U.S. citizen or resident. If you become a U.S. citizen, notify the IRS that the QDOT tax no longer applies. You must file IRS Form 706 QDT.

7.9 Qualified terminable interest property (QTIP) trust

A qualified terminable interest property (QTIP) trust provides a surviving spouse with the rights to all trust income during his or her life, but does not allow for assets to be sold or removed. Upon the death of the surviving spouse, the trust assets pass on to an alternate party named by the grantor, such as children or grandchildren. A corporate trustee for management of the funds and distributions usually controls the trust assets.

The QTIP trust helps ensure the passing on of assets to the rightful heirs. It is commonly used for previous marriages with multiple beneficiaries. The donor can provide income for the surviving spouse and ensure that his or her children will receive their inheritance upon the death of the second spouse.

If you make the QTIP election, the assets are taxable to the estate. If you make a QTIP equivalent trust, the assets are removed from the estate.

To qualify a QTIP trust for the non-marital tax exclusion, you must make a special election (Form 706) on your federal estate tax return. The property from the QTIP trust is included in the surviving spouse's gross estate, so you will need to make final arrangements as to how you want funds distributed (i.e., rolled into a irrevocable trust, spendthrift trust, special needs trust, or educational trust).

The advantage of the QTIP trust is that the grantor can control where his or her money will go upon death. However, unlike in a non-marital trust, the surviving spouse controls the money during his or her lifetime.

In a QTIP trust, the trust income must be vested in the surviving spouse only. If the surviving spouse does not need the income, he or she can elect to distribute the fund assets as so desired, or as specified in the trust documents. Upon the death of the surviving spouse, the trust assets pass directly to the named beneficiaries.

The QTIP trust can be named the beneficiary of an individual retirement account (IRA). This could provide the surviving spouse with access to retirement plan funds through an independent trustee to ensure professional investment advice. It would protect assets from controversy from second marriages or divorce and insure that any remaining assets are distributed to the ultimate beneficiaries made by the donor. It will also qualify for the estate tax marital deduction and satisfy the 70½ mandatory distribution requirements.

When establishing a QTIP trust (or any trust), it is best to discuss the terms with your spouse and family so that everyone understands what it is and what it does. Consider using corporate trustees to manage and distribute funds on behalf of your family for housing, income, and education. Be specific when discussing your succession goals with your attorney.

7.10 Testamentary trusts

A testamentary trust (inter vivos) is a trust written inside a will. The will goes to probate then comes back to the trust. The surviving spouse then applies for a federal EIN to fund the decedent's trust. The trust can be revocable or irrevocable at death. Generally it is written with two wills — his and hers or an A will/trust and a B will/trust — to take advantage of the unified credit deduction.

To avoid this type of situation, it would have been easier to set up a revocable and amendable living trust, which would receive a step-up in basis on all assets at the time of both the first and the second death. Because the trust owns the assets, there is no need for appraisals of any assets (unless you were selling). As well, because a revocable trust is considered a grantor trust, it is thus taxed to the grantor rather than to the trust and there are no special tax filing requirements.

7.11 Spendthrift trusts

A spendthrift trust provides income or assets to a person but restricts the amount of money he or she can spend. It may also

Non-marital tax exclusion: *The non-marital tax exclusion is used when all assets from your estate are transferred to your surviving spouse. It avoids estate taxes, but is fully taxable in the surviving spouse's estate. It is best to place the non-marital deduction into a B trust, otherwise you will lose that amount of the unified credit.*

Example

Mr. and Mrs. X held property jointly inside a testamentary trust. They had two wills/trusts to split assets and take advantage of the credit shelter trust.

Mr. X died first. Unfortunately, his trust did not provide for a power of attorney for his wife. They had no successor trustees, only contingent trustees (who happened to be their children).

Mrs. X had several problems: Mr. X's will came back from probate with a half step-up in basis on his half of the property (because the testamentary trust is still irrevocable). Mrs. X had full value (because she has not yet died). When Mrs. X wanted to sell the property, she had to receive written permission from her children (the contingent trustees) and had to pay capital gains on her half of the property.

specify the time when the funds may be distributed. The money is generally removed from creditor reach.

These trusts are commonly used in bankruptcy cases where the money is kept from creditors even if the beneficiary files for Chapter 7 of the Bankruptcy Code. However, if the beneficiary receives the money from a life insurance or trust within 180 days of the donor's death, the full amount may come back into the bankrupt estate. Check with a bankruptcy attorney for further explanation, as this is a complicated area.

7.12 Special needs trust

A special needs trust is an irrevocable trust established for individuals who may not be able to take care of themselves. The trust is generally funded with life insurance to provide the necessary funds for the proper care or facilities needed.

When you fund the special needs trust, the Medicaid division will want to review the trust documents and approve them before they become effective. Some states are making this review mandatory to make sure the trust is properly established and administered (as well as not taking advantage of Medicaid). Further, Medicaid in some states is collecting any funds that were supplied by Medicaid in support of the individual prior to final funding.

7.13 Defective grantor trusts (Irrevocable defective income trust)

Defective grantor trusts are designed for the benefit of your family so that all the income and principal of the trust inure the benefit of the family. The donor pays taxes on all income to the trust, thus reducing the taxable estate. By paying the tax on all income to the trust, you are making gifts to the family, but these indirect gifts become gift and estate tax free under the current law.

For example, if you sell a highly appreciated asset you pay a capital gain on the profit. If you sell the asset to the defective grantor trust, there is no gain to pay. The trust would pay for the assets by installment to the seller, funded by the income generated in the trust. All future assets and growth are removed from your estate for the benefit of your family. If you elect to no longer pay the income taxes, you relinquish all rights of income and the trust or beneficiaries then pay the taxes.

7.14 Disclaimer trusts

A disclaimer trust is a trust in a will that leaves substantial amounts to the surviving spouse. It is generally used to substitute as a credit shelter trust and take advantage of the unified credit when only a single will is in effect. This provision is for those who have not taken advantage of the "A" and "B" trust provisions.

The trust becomes effective only when the surviving spouse disclaims some or all of the property left to the surviving spouse. This means that the beneficiary may refuse or accept a bequest under the terms of the will or trust. A person who disclaims is regarded by the IRS to have never received the property. It passes to the next recipient and, therefore, is not federally taxed. The spouse has nine months from the death to disclaim any money or property.

7.15 Rabbi trust (deferred compensation)

In 1996, the IRS issued a private letter ruling to a New York synagogue that wanted to provide a supplemental retirement for its rabbi. The ruling permitted the trust to be tax deferred and not include current income. This started a new compensation plan known as the rabbi trust.

A rabbi trust is a non-qualified deferred compensation program. It does not come under the federal pension rules (Employee Retirement Income Security Act or ERISA).

The trust can be funded or unfunded. Back loading (unfunded) is attractive for corporations because they do not have to fund any assets into the trust until something triggers the event. However, the funds must remain subject to creditor control and the trusts run the risk of default when distributions are made for retirement, as the company needs to have the money to place into the trust.

The corporation pays taxes before funding the trust, must pay FICA/FUTA upon funding, and must make elections in the prior year for contributions. Usually a percentage of salary, bonus, or 1099 (must be compensation) are elected. Dividends are not allowed to fund a rabbi trust.

1099: *Untaxed income from any source. It could include income from dividends, capital gains, or self-employment where no tax is withheld (i.e., commissioned salespeople).*

Rabbi and deferred compensation trusts are popular in large C corporations to use discretionary powers to attract or keep key employees. If at retirement the plan distributes funds to the employee, it will be treated as ordinary income. Generally, they are used when benefits may be at risk from failure of the business or ownership control. The corporation receives no tax deduction to the trust, but will receive tax deductions to the beneficiaries designated by the trust upon distribution. Only C corporations can take advantage of any deferred compensation plans. Check with a retirement plan specialist to see if this type of plan meets your particular need.

Deferred compensation plans, such as Rabbi trusts, also offer an alternative to paying the 15% excise tax. The C corporation can elect to defer an unlimited amount of compensation to elected employees and match the contribution if so desired. There is no deduction for the employer until the distribution is made to the participant of the trust.

The corporation pays corporate tax before funding of the trust. They must also pay FICA/FUTA at the time of funding. The corporation pays taxes on the amount of income, capital gains, and dividends made by the trust.

C corporation: *A legal entity as identified by the IRS that pays dividends, has shareholders, a board of directors, and stock. Unlike an S corporation or limited liability company, the C corporation must pay tax on income and before dividend distribution.*

Usually the trust is invested in growth stocks, growth mutual funds, municipal bonds, corporate-owned life insurance (COLI), or some other income tax–free bonds. Each year the contribution is made, the employee must make the election of how this deferred income will be taken. You can take the deferral in the following year or take income at a certain date in the future (e.g., after 10 years). Upon distribution, the corporation receives a tax deduction, and the recipient is taxed as ordinary income in the year it is taken.

7.16 Offshore trusts

Offshore trusts are trusts designed to offset U.S. taxation. When it sounds too good to be true, it probably is. Offshore trusts are the target of the IRS criminal investigation unit, and boast some 125 or more abusive trust practices. Even if an offshore trust is legitimate, when you bring money back into the United States, you still need to report it and pay taxes. Better alternatives are charitable remainder trusts, fixed gift annuities, annuities, life insurance, deferred compensation plans, and family limited partnerships.

7.17 Family limited partnerships (FLP)

Family limited partnerships (FLPs) are designed for families that want to keep their business in the family. Discounts allow more units (e.g., stocks and assets) to be distributed to family members.

A word of caution about these: IRS rules are very specific, and a lot of abuse has taken place over the years. If you gift into the FLP to family members below the 70% appraised fair market value determined by the IRS, you will have to pay back taxes (55% gift tax from the date of value) and penalties of 200% or more.

The IRS has issued several Technical Advice Memoranda disallowing valuation discounts. Typically, if you use separate bank accounts, tax returns, reasonable compensation, competent appraisers, and liquidity of the donor's interest, you should have no problems.

Here's how FLPs work: If you had $1 million (equal to 1 million limited units) in property and securities, and you gifted 11,000 limited units to a child, the amount of the gift with discounts would probably be $7,700 (appraised value is 70% of the gifted amount of $11,000). Effectively you could give away more units without violating the gift exclusion. The IRS will eventually test buyer/seller willingness to sell for declared amounts of the value each owns of the partnership.

Note: In a critical ruling by the IRS on March 22, 2002, the tax court has rejected claims of gifts using the annual exclusion under IRC sec. 2503(b) to limited liability companies and family limited partnerships. This may become quite dramatic on its outcome if it clears the Appellate Court. The IRS claims it does not convey a substantial present economic interest. It may become necessary to pay current income to qualify for the annual gift exclusion. The three-year look-back provision will probably apply as long as you meet all the requirements stated above and there is no abuse to the trust.

7.18 Total return trusts

Most trusts require the trustee to distribute all the principal and income to the beneficiary. The total return trust is a unitrust that distributes a certain percentage of the trust to the beneficiaries. If the trust grows in value, the income to the beneficiary grows also. If the trust does not generate enough income, the trustee can sell assets and reinvest to produce the income desired.

The advantage of selling assets inside the trust is that the tax is capital gains tax, not ordinary income tax. When the trust terminates, the heirs can take advantage of the appreciation of assets. This has advantages over an income trust in that the total return trust relieves the trustee discipline in investing in a balanced portfolio and allows investing based on long-term performance.

7.19 Dynasty trust

A dynasty trust is designed to pass on large life insurance proceeds to intended beneficiaries regardless of the taxation to the main estate. With the laws of perpetuity dissolved in most states (the trust now can last forever) dynasty trusts become very attractive to the wealthy. You buy a large life insurance policy (typically with a single premium), and place it into a dynasty trust on behalf of your children. You typically borrow the money to pay the life insurance premium to avoid gift tax.

Dynasty trusts are generally designed to pass on an inheritance to your children. Other beneficiaries could be subject to inheritance taxes on the portion they receive.

Upon death, the named beneficiaries receive income tax-free and estate tax-free money regardless of the federal estate taxes, income taxes, and death taxes born unto the main estate. The money is usually placed into another trust to provide income, education, housing, or any other specific control.

7.20 2503(b) trust

2503(b) trusts are required to pay all income from the trust to the beneficiaries. The crummy trust gives the beneficiaries the right to withdraw the income. Having the right of withdrawal makes the gift a present interest and qualifies the gift for the annual exclusion ($11,000 per person).

7.21 2503(c) trust

A 2503(c) trust is established for the benefit of a minor. The income can be paid out or accumulated. Income that is accumulated is taxed to the trust. If the income is paid out, it is taxable to the minor. Any gifts to the trust must qualify for the annual exclusion. All principal and income must be made available to the minor at attained age or no later than age 21.

7.22 Charitable lead trust (CLT) [IRC 170(f)(2)(b)]

Charitable gifting is rewarding both internally (feeling good) as well as externally (financially).

A charitable lead trust is an irrevocable trust that distributes income to a charity now for a specified period of time. The donor is responsible for trust income. You receive a tax deduction off your current income, and upon death, the trust distributes the remainder of the assets to the beneficiaries. These are the same as wealth replacement trusts set up for replacement of assets that go to charity. The estate is granted a deduction for the value actuarially assumed to pass to the charity during this period.

Similar to the CLT is the FLIP trust where income goes to the charity for a specified period of time, and at the end of the term the trust flips back to the donor or beneficiaries. The donor must decide at the time the trust is established where the money is going. Common uses for an FLIP are for IRAs when the donor does not need the income and would like to offset the triple taxation (federal, state, and local income tax; state death taxes; and federal estate taxes) from non-distributed qualified plans.

Attained age: In most states the attained age is 18 for men and 21 for women.

7.23 Charitable remainder trust (CRT) [IRS publication 526 REV December 2000]

A charitable remainder trust (CRT) is generally used to reduce federal estate tax. It removes assets from your estate (usually highly appreciated assets like stocks, mutual funds, and real estate that have a low cost basis) and moves them into a trust. In return, you avoid gift tax, defer capital gains, receive a tax deduction on current income, and at some future date receive income for life.

You establish a wealth replacement trust (life insurance) to replace the "remainder" of assets that go to a charity named in the trust upon death of both spouses. The policy is usually placed into an irrevocable life insurance trust (ILIT), and is income tax free as well as estate tax free. You can distribute the money into another trust and provide income and education for your beneficiaries according to the direction outlined in the irrevocable trust.

The tax deductions and income are based on an IRS formula. This gift of assets entitles you to a tax deduction from your current income. This deduction is calculated based on age at the time of the gift. It allows you to take 30% of your adjusted gross income (AGI) over a six-year period off your income tax. You must take the maximum amount each year until it is exhausted. Each time you "gift" you receive the same treatment. If you gift cash to the trust, you can deduct up to 50% of your AGI over six years at the maximum amount each year.

Any amount gifted to the trust is removed from your estate for federal estate tax purposes. The idea is to reduce assets below the federal unified tax credit. See Chapter 4 for more information.

In return, you receive income for you and your spouse — generally for life. Part of this income is made up of capital gains and ordinary income (your income at the time of receipt), and part may be tax free.

Assets moved into a charitable remainder trust can be property, artwork, stocks, bonds, jewelry, or mutual funds — generally assets that are low cost basis and provide very little income. The idea is to transfer low income-producing assets into higher, creditor-protected income for life.

The charity must meet the definition of a qualified charity under IRS code Section 501(c)(3) (see below) and pass the 5% probability rule (i.e., the donation must retain at least 5% of corpus after the calculations for distribution to the donor). The interest must outlast the beneficiary before the charity can receive the remainder of funds.

There are two types of charitable remainder trusts:

- *Fixed:* Charitable remainder annuity trusts (CRAT) provide a fixed-dollar amount equal to at least 5% of the assets placed into the trust. No additional contributions are allowed. It provides predictable cash flow, and income must be paid out each year. No annual evaluations are needed.
- *Variable:* Charitable remainder unitrusts (CRUT) provide income based on a fixed percentage — generally not less than 5% of the trust's assets (revalued annually). Additional contributions are allowed. Cash flow rises or falls with annual evaluations and it does not require income to be paid out each year.

Corpus: *The principal property of a trust.*

Net income charitable remainder unitrusts (NIMCRUT) are designed for income at a later date. Additional contributions are allowed. The investments can include rent, dividends, royalties, stocks, and bonds. These are typically used by people who are deferring the income to a later date (i.e., they want to add more over time, and do not yet need the income).

7.24 How to determine which charities qualify for deductible charitable contributions

To receive a tax deduction for contributions, the charity you donate to must be qualified under IRS Section 501(c)(3) of the tax code. Contributions to the following entities are considered a proper charitable contribution:

- Churches, temples, other religious organizations
- Federal, state, and local governments if the contribution is for public purposes
- Non-profit hospitals and schools
- Red Cross, Goodwill Industries, Boy Scouts, Girl Scouts, Salvation Army
- Public parks and recreation facilities
- War veterans' organizations
- Out-of-pocket expenses for an individual who serves for a qualified organization as a volunteer

Non-deductible contributions include the following:

- Individuals
- Tuition
- Value of time and services
- Political groups or candidates for public office
- Foreign organizations
- Sports clubs, labor unions, chambers of commerce, civic leagues
- Dues or bills for country clubs, lodges, fraternal organizations
- Raffle tickets, lottery tickets, bingo
- Homeowners' associations, lobbyists, or groups for profit

Table 14 illustrates the results of gifting. It uses the current tax laws and is not designed to indicate investment performance. This illustration has been created based on current tax laws, which may be subject to change.

Remember to keep a record of any charitable donation over $250. You should also receive a written receipt from the charity.

Trusts

7.25 Generation skipping transfer tax trust (GSTT)

A generation skipping transfer tax trust (GSTT) is an irrevocable trust designed to "skip" a generation. Grandchildren are generally the recipients of the trust. Everybody has a $1 million exemption (indexed to inflation) to gift into his or her GSTT.

Table 14: Charitable remainder trust gifting: Cash flow projections from unitrust

Year	1st Age	2nd Age	Contribution to unitrust	Unitrust value	Gross income	Net income*	Income tax deduction**	Tax savings	Net cash flow
1	60	65	$5,000,000	$5,062,133	$269,589	$162,832	$230,877	$91,427	$254,259
2	61	66		5,163,376	404,971	244,602	271,491	107,511	352,113
3	62	67		5,266,644	413,070	249,494	273,921	108,473	357,967
4	63	68		5,371,979	421,332	254,484	169,211	67,008	321,492
5	64	69		5,479,416	429,758				259,574
6	65	70		5,589,004	438,353				264,765
7	66	71		5,700,785	447,120				270,061
8	67	72		5,814,800	456,063				275,462
9	68	73		5,931,096	465,184				280,971
10	69	74		6,049,718	474,488				286,591
11	70	75		6,170,712	483,977				292,322
12	71	76		6,294,127	493,657				298,169
13	72	77		6,420,009	503,530				304,132
14	73	78		6,548,409	513,601				310,215
15	74	79		6,679,378	523,873				316,419
16	75	80		6,812,965	534,390				322,749
17	76	81		6,949,244	545,037				329,202
18	77	82		7,088,209	555,938				335,787
19	78	83		7,229,973	567,057				342,502
20	79***			7,374,573	578,398				349,352

Table 14 — Continued

21	80			7,522,064	589,966				356,339
22	81			7,672,505	601,765				363,466
23	82			7,825,955	613,800				370,735
24	83			7,982,475	626,076				378,150
25	84			*8,142,124*****	638,598				386,713

* Net income is a blend of deferred capital gains and ordinary income tax.

** Tax deduction was based on appreciated property (30% of AGI) sold from the trust, and must be taken over a period of six years, with the maximum amount each year.

- Output (income % of Unitrust) was 10%; growth rate was based on 15%.
- Does not include payments to the Wealth Replacement Trust (Life Insurance Policy, which can be paid from the trust).

***Assumes one spouse dies balance of payments to surviving spouse.

**** The amount to replace to beneficiaries is $8,142,124 going to charity. You could buy a single premium policy, or a variable second-to-die policy with an increasing death benefit. As an illustration based on Female age 60, preferred health with the husband as the second insured, the trust is the owner of the policy; premiums paid by the trust on an annual basis of $67,800 with an increasing death benefit, the investment hypothetical return was used at 12% growth. The replacement value of the Life Insurance going to the beneficiaries would be approximately $10,302,661.

You can apply this to your marital deduction trust (A/B credit shelter) so that you can take advantage of both GSTT contributions. The money allocated is not subject to creditors, divorce, or court orders since the donor does not own the assets. Anything over the allocation amount (except the growth) is subject to the 55% taxation.

The beneficiaries generally receive an income interest or an income specified in the trust instrument. The GSTT is in addition to your unified credit. See Chapter 4 for more information on the unified credit.

Generally the gift tax applies to any gift of real or personal property, whether tangible or intangible, that you made directly, indirectly, in trust, or by any other means to a donee.

The state of New Jersey repealed the laws of perpetuity (the old law was a carry over from our English predecessors) on July 9, 1999. The laws of perpetuity meant that a trust could last forever. With the repeal, true dynasty trusts can be established or transferred. Consult with a tax attorney on the new rules, and the conditions of grandfathered trusts to new trusts.

Beware of the Delaware tax trap: the original rule against perpetuities applied to trusts created by the exercise of power of appointment rather than at the time of the trust creation. This allowed a perpetual trust by exercising successive powers of appointment. The IRS rules that if you exercise the power of appointment, including a limited power to create another power of appointment that suspends absolute ownership or alienation of the property without regard for the creation of the first power, it could cause the property to be included in the decedent's gross estate. This obviously could trigger estate and gift tax consequences transferring to the New Jersey power of appointment.

Proper GSTT funding and allocations should be made with an experienced tax attorney familiar with the laws of the state you live in. See Diagram 3 for a generation-skipping strategy using a number of different trusts.

Diagram 3: Generation skipping strategy

Revocable living trust (RLT): No probate	**Irrevocable life insurance (ILIT):** Income tax free and estate tax free	**Qualified personal residence trust (QPRT)** removes resident property from the estate	**Crummy trust:** gifting $22,000 per year per child (GST allocation)
	Credit shelter trust A $1 million (exemption 2002)	**Credit shelter trust B** $1 million (exemption 2002)	

$2 million exemption from estate taxes

Family trusts: Assets taxed on the amount above the unified credit for federal estate taxes; no capital gains or gift tax (the grandchildren are taxed)

GST shelters $2,2 million (basis) tax free for grandchildren using crummy trust at $22,000 per year or lump sum during lifetime or at death

This strategy removes most of your federal taxable estate and avoids probate, gift tax, and capital gains tax. It provides for your family and grandchildren with future income according to your family trust. The GST exemption for 2002 is $1,1 million each, in addition to the unified credit exemption.

7.26 Retirement plans and GSTT taxation

An area of unbelievable taxation on qualified plans exists when you try to use them for generation skipping. The plan will be taxed at three federal levels (and probably state death taxes, which disappear in 2005, but will probably be replaced with some other tax):

- Federal estate taxes at 50% (starts decreasing in 2002 and resorts back to 55% in 2011 under the sunset rule)
- Generation skipping transfer tax (GSTT) at 50%
- State death tax
- Lump sum income tax on retirement distributions after death (federal income tax, state income tax, and any local income tax). The qualified plan has been pre-tax dollars and growing tax deferred, so no income tax has been withheld. Some states tax your qualified plan on every contribution, so state income tax may not be due.

Assuming you don't need the income from the qualified plan, you may consider the following alternatives to GSST transfers:

- Roll the qualified plan to an individual retirement rollover account (IRRA). This will allow a surviving spouse to assume the qualified plan under his or her social security number and convert it to a Stretch IRA. The Stretch IRA stretches the period of tax deferral on earnings over multiple generations (and the IRS allows various life expectancies of beneficiaries, such as children and grandchildren).
- Gift the plan to a charitable remainder trust (CRT), taking a tax deduction, and receiving income which you can pass on to your children. Life insurance can be used to replace the gift with tax-free and estate tax-free money. The CRT can pay the life insurance premiums.
- Take a lump sum distribution and only pay the income tax due, transferred to your surviving spouse or trust.
- Set up a Roth IRA, which can now be used in 401K Roth deferred plans.
- Use life insurance (ILIT) to cover the tax loss and pass on to your beneficiaries federal tax free and income tax free dollars.

8. Strategies for Estate Planning Using Trusts

Understanding how to combine trust applications can be quite perplexing. Let's look at how John and Jane Doe decided to use various trust strategies. They were concerned with transferring the maximum amount of wealth to their children, providing income for themselves in retirement, and in the event John passed away before Jane, minimizing estate taxes, keeping their primary residence in the family, and avoiding probate. Their estate was worth $7 million in liquid assets, plus their $2 million home. Based on the assumption that John would die first, they —

A revocable living trust can hold your home, bank accounts, broker accounts, out-of-state properties, certificates of deposits, bonds, jewelry, artwork, antiques, collectibles, and anything else of value.

- funded a revocable living trust (Trust A, post QTIP Equivalent) to hold all assets, and avoid probate (**Note**: Remember that a QTIP election must be made at time the trust is established and becomes taxable in the estate. The QTIP equivalent is not an election and is not included in the gross estate for federal estate tax purposes.);

- prepared durable powers of attorney for health care, as well as financial proxies, living wills, and credit shelter trusts (these are separate documents prepared in addition to trusts or wills);

- created a 10-year term QPRT residence trust to remove the property from the estate, (applying the unified credit; see section 7.6, this chapter) (when the term expired, they paid fair market value rent to the children);

- placed John's $2-million life insurance policy into an irrevocable life insurance trust (see section 7.3, this chapter) and paid it with a single premium (upon John's death, $1 million, estate- and income-tax free, would go into the QTIP equivalent trust to provide income for Jane and protect the corpus for his heirs);

- arranged that upon John's death, they would fund the B trust (see section 7.5, this chapter) using a sprinkle provision with $1 million for the future benefit of the children (or additional income for Jane); it remains estate-tax free forever regardless of growth (except in certain states that will tax the difference between the federal exemption and the state exemption they declare);

- gifted $5 million to a charitable remainder trust to provide income for both (see section 7.23, this chapter) and additional income for Jane if John dies first; and

- purchased a $5 million second-to-die life insurance policy for the children to replace the $5 million that would go to charity after John and Jane both died. The $5 million dollar gift to the charitable remainder trust was used to reduce the estate to $2 million for estate tax purposes (after deducting the unified credit, the estate tax due is zero), and to supply a charitable tax deduction against current income. The life insurance is estate/income tax-free.

In summary, on John's death —

- the A trust passes the balance of assets to Jane without taxation or probate (UN-limited marital trust),
- the B trust takes advantage of the unified credit (by-pass trust/credit shelter trust),
- the C trust (QTIP equivalent) houses assets to provide income for Jane and protect the corpus for their heirs,
- the QPRT real estate remains in the family, and
- the CRT income flows to Jane.

Beneficiaries have the right to replace the corporate trustee with another person if the trustee does not perform satisfactorily.

All the life insurance is estate- and income-tax free. After Jane's death all the assets (including the $5 million second-to-die insurance policy) are transferred income- and estate-tax free* to the irrevocable family income trust, which is managed by the corporate trustee selected prior to her death. (The beneficiaries have the right to replace the corporate trustee if he or she does not perform.) The corporate trustee elected will pay trust taxes, provide an income stream to the beneficiaries, make tax filings, and provide education and housing to the children, grandchildren, and will manage the investments in accordance with the trust documents. As long as the investments remain in the trust, the beneficiaries will pay income tax only on distributions.

There are specific requirements you must meet if you use strategies such as these. Consult your accountant, tax attorney, or financial advisor for more information. The above example is provided for illustration only.

Taxation continues to go up, not down, and creating strategies to distribute your wealth takes planning, time, effort, and research. The time to implement a plan is now.

---

* *(The A Trust or assets held directly in Jane's name or her estate may be subject to estate taxes if the aggregate exceeds the then current unified credit.)*

9. Taxation of Trusts

Trusts and estates are taxed very quickly at the highest rate. Table 15 shows the tax payable on trust income.

Table 15: Tax on trust income

Taxable income from trusts	Tax
$0-$1,850	15%
$1,850-$4,400	$277.50 plus 27% of excess over $1,850
$4,400-$6,750	$966.00 plus 30% of excess over $4,400
$6,750-$9,200	$1,671 plus 35% of excess over $6,750
$9,200+	$2,528.50 plus 38.6% of excess over $9,200

The Uniform Gifts to Minors Act is a way of transferring property to a minor without the use of a trust. You can use a lifetime gift ($11,000) or transfer by will.

The act allows gifts to include cash, securities, real estate, and royalties. The child cannot take possession until 21 (in some states, the age of possession is 25).

Taxes are payable on these transfers:

- First $750   Tax $0
- Next $750   Current child's rate
- Over $1500   Parent's tax rate

Parents may elect to file Form 8814 to report the interest and dividends for children under age 14 on their Form 1040 if the child had interest and dividend income between $700 and $7000 and had no federal income tax withheld. A separate Form 8814 must be used with each child. Keep in mind this will adjust your adjusted gross income. Alternatively, you can use Form 8615 if the child has more than $1,500 of unearned income (Form 8615 will help compute the child tax).

10. Private Foundations

The IRS rules divide organizations into two classifications: private foundations and public charities. A private operating foundation is any private foundation that spends at least 85% of its adjusted net income or its minimum investment return, whichever is less, directly for the active conduct of its exempt activities. Also, the donor may take advantage of 50% of contributions to the private foundation up to 50% of adjusted gross income.

A public charity generally receives broad public support, and is thus not considered a private foundation. These are organizations such as:

- Churches
- Schools
- Hospitals
- Government
- Publicly supported organizations

Private foundations are required to file Form 990-PF or Form 5227 annual return. Even if you are waiting for approval for your private foundation you should file the return. Split interest trusts section 4947(a)(2) of the code must file Form 5227. An excise tax is imposed on the net investment income of most domestic private foundations.

The foundation must apply for exempt status from the IRS before the foundation is exempt from federal income taxation and before contributions to the foundation will be deductible. Once incorporated, the foundation must file the following:

- Form 1023 (application for recognition of exemption)
- Form 8718 (user fee for exempt organizations determination letter request)
- Form SS-4 (application for employer identification number)

A private foundation must file duplicate originals of the foundation's Articles of Incorporation with the state. The secretary of state will record one of the copies with the local registrar of deeds and issue a Certificate of Incorporation if the articles comply with the applicable corporate law. Once it is incorporated, the foundation can do business and elect the board of directors. At that time the board can consider the long-term investment and distribution policies of the foundation.

The donor may control the foundation, but must not engage in self-dealing. Self-dealing includes loans, payments or excessive compensation, preferential availability of services, purchases or sales, and diversions of income to disqualified persons. Also, the donor must be cautious of risky or speculative investments that would jeopardize the charitable purpose of the foundation. The combined holdings of a private foundation and all disqualified persons generally may not exceed 20% of the voting control in any corporation conducting business that is not substantially related to the exempt purpose of the foundation.

11. Funding Forms

When setting up a trust, you will need a variation of funding forms for —

- Trust amendment form, assignment form
- Change beneficiary for life insurance, annuities
- Change beneficiary for IRA, 401K, pension plans

You'll also need a letter of transfer for —

- Stock, bonds, mutual funds, certificates of deposit
- Letter of instruction and transfer for your bank and brokerage accounts
- Schedule A, B, C
- Letter for transfer of your land trust (deed) to your revocable trust (the bank must approve transfer before you can record new deed at the county office of records)
- Bill of sale

Most funding forms can be obtained from your attorney to meet your specific need. See the Resources section at the back of this book for a list of forms needed for filing income and expenses for a decedent. Worksheet 9 provides a generic outline to help you understand the requirements for changing your assets into your trust.

There are a lot of rules for foundations. Consult an attorney who can help establish a private or public foundation. It's a great way to establish your legacy and help out some great causes.

Worksheet 9: Typical forms outline

I, _____, of the City of _____, County of _____, State of _____, do hereby transfer, sell, and assign all rights, titles and interest without consideration which I have in:

_____

_____

_____

To my Revocable and Amendable Living Trust, _____ (name of trust), dated_____ with _____ Trustees.

In Witness whereof, we have signed this assignment document on this

Day of _____ month _____ and year _____

_____

Name of grantor

_____

Name of grantor

Certificate of Acknowledgement of Notary Public

States of   )

         : Ss

County of   )

On this_____day of_____, _____, appeared before me_____, personally known to me (or proved to me on the basis of satisfactory evidence) to be the persons whose names are subscribed in this instrument, and acknowledged that they executed it.

_____

Notary Public

(SEAL)

Trusts

6
UNDERSTANDING YOUR INVESTMENTS

This section discusses various investments, including mutual funds, life insurance, annuities, Section 529 college funding programs, and bonds. By understanding your risk tolerance, the taxation of investments, and how their commission structures work, you will be better able to maximize your assets.

1. How Do I Choose An Advisor?

More and more people today are choosing to use a professional to advise them on their investments. Not only does it save time, but professionals also make it their business to stay current. Choose your investment advisor carefully and know with whom you are dealing. This is becoming difficult with all the players today: banks are brokers, brokers are banks, accountants are brokers, and now, insurance companies are not only brokers, but banks.

Ask your potential financial advisor the following questions, and remember to get (and check out) referrals:

- What are your qualifications?
- What licenses do you hold?
- Do you sell more than just mutual funds and annuities?

- Do you have an investment policy? For example, how often do you complete reviews on investments? Do you have a strict investment discipline by risk tolerance?

You can also check out advisors on the Web. For a list of complaints and grievances against brokers, as well as their education and employment history, visit <www.NASD.com>. You can also check directly with the Department of Insurance.

When choosing an investment, always read the prospectus and know what you are buying. Make sure it fits your risk tolerance, time frame, tax efficiency, and liquidity, and confirm any sales charges you will pay. You can check out mutual funds costs on <www.andrewtobias.com> or <www.morningstar.com>.

The National Association of Securities Dealers (NASD) states Rule 405 that the broker must "know thy client." I say to you, "Know thy broker."

Once you have made an investment, make sure that your money and policies or investments are in fact secured. If you buy auto insurance, life insurance, or homeowners insurance, call the carrier directly after you secure a policy from an agent to make sure that your money and policies are there.

2. I Have Social Security. Why Do I Need to Invest?

Most people do not save enough money for their retirement, and rely on social security as their main source of income. A recent study by the Department of Human Services uncovered the following information based on every 100 people retiring at age 65:

- 23 people will need to continue working
- 73 people will rely on others for support
- Only 4 people will retire comfortably

Ask yourself, "Will social security be there for me when I retire?" and, "At what age will it kick in?" Think about the following:

- The age to collect social security is rising.
- Over 42% of retirees rely on social security for income.
- The average benefit in 2002 was $852 per month.
- In 2000, an estimated one out of three people were on social security. By 2030, it could be as high as one to one.
- Company pension plans are all but disappearing, or reducing benefits.

Remember, if you are between 62 and 64, you will have to take a retirement earnings test to qualify for benefits. To learn more about how wages prior to age 65 apply to your social security benefits, go to < www.ssa.gov >, and select "Retirement planner," then select "Calculators."

Consider, also, whether health benefits are part of your plan when you retire. If not, check out what it will cost to replace this very important resource, or if there is a cost with your employer if it is part of your plan. The age to receive full social security benefits is rising. Using social security as a guideline, you need to examine other investment options to supplement the shortfalls of income that you may encounter for retirement. See Chapter 7 for more information on long-term care policies.

3. Calculating Your Risk Tolerance

There's no doubt that playing the stock market can be risky. However, a number of lower risk investments are available that beat leaving your money under your mattress. The returns may not be as attractive as the higher risk investments, but if your risk tolerance is low or you are just starting to invest, you may be more comfortable with a low-risk investment. To make the most of your investment portfolio and be comfortable with the level of risk you are taking, use Worksheet 10 to help you calculate your tolerance for risk.

Ask your financial planner to run illustrations for your retirement based on the information you have completed in Chapters 1 and 2.

Worksheet 10: Calculating Risk versus Reward

Current age
1. College funding desired: $ _____
2. Date desired for retirement: $ _____
3. Dollars needed for retirement (indexed to inflation): $ _____
4. Current dollars saved: $ _____

Most of this information can be obtained from a financial advisor or on the Internet. You can insert your numbers on their calculators and they will tell you your shortfalls and how much additional money you need to save in each category.

Different investment allocation choices result in different fluctuations in value of portfolios. Most people do not do better investing on their own (as opposed to an experienced advisor).

Worksheet 10 — Continued

What is your current allocation of investments?

Cash	____%	Stock	____%
Fixed income	____%	Annuities	____%
CDs	____%	International	____%
Real estate	____%	Other	____%

What is your involvement with the decision-making process of your investments? _____

What is your experience with investments?

Stocks___ Bonds___ Mutual funds___ Options___ Annuites___ CDs___ REITs___

Using the following questions, let's see where your risk and reward tolerances lie:

1. Strongly disagree
2. Slightly disagree
3. Neutral
4. Slightly agree
5. Strongly agree

I am willing to accept greater price volatility in return for potentially higher long-term gains.
    Circle 1 2 3 4 5

Generating a return that offsets the effect of inflation is very important to me.
    Circle 1 2 3 4 5

I do not need current income from my investments.   Circle 1 2 3 4 5

My investment goals are long term (greater than 7 years).   Circle 1 2 3 4 5

I am generally a risk taker.   Circle 1 2 3 4 5

I am generally not a risk taker.   Circle 1 2 3 4 5

I am willing to bear an above average level of risk, and can accept years of negative returns.
    Circle 1 2 3 4 5

I do not need to convert my investments into cash; I have enough liquid assets to meet my expenses.
    Circle 1 2 3 4 5

If I invested $10,000 in a long term investment six months ago, and its current value is now $8500, I would probably keep the investment.   Circle 1 2 3 4 5

The higher the number, the more risk you are willing to take. Most people fall within the following asset allocation categories:

- **Conservative:** Safety of principal is my main objective. Minimal risk.
- **Conservative to moderate:** Safety of principal is my primary objective, but my secondary objective is growth of capital.

Worksheet 10 — Continued

- **Moderate:** Growth of capital and safety of principal are both important. Moderate risk is acceptable to increase capital appreciation.

- **Moderate to aggressive:** Growth of capital is my primary objective. A secondary goal is safety of principal. A fair amount of risk is acceptable to take advantage of greater growth opportunities.

- **Aggressive:** Growth of capital is the primary objective. High risk is acceptable in seeking superior returns.

Generally, most people fall into a moderate investment attitude (around a 3 to 4). Balanced portfolios may be a better idea for these individuals. Have your financial advisor show you numbers that will illustrate the asset allocation or check out <www.morningstar.com>, <www.yahoofinance.com>, or <www.investinginbonds.com>.

For example, if your total score from the questions above was between 17 and 22, you might consider 30% money market, 30% fixed income, and 40% equities. If your score was 29–34, you might consider 10% cash, 10% fixed income, and 80% equities. You need to match your goals to your investment risk, available investable income, and time frame.

Remember that all investments have some form or element of risk (e.g., CDs may not keep up with inflation, stocks may lose value, bonds can default).

Common sense, organization, and research are your best protection for safeguarding your money and investments. Know what you are buying and the risks associated with it.

Once you know your risk tolerance, you will have a better idea of what kinds of investments you'll feel most comfortable with. Most funds have specific objectives. Work with your financial advisor to choose the type of fund best suited to your assets, long-term plans, and risk tolerance.

- Growth funds accumulate wealth over time and accept price volatility. The average goal is an 8% to 10% annual return.

- Aggressive growth funds try to achieve above average growth over time, but they accept substantial risk in trying to achieve growth of 10% or greater.

Understanding Your Investments **87**

- Income/growth funds balance their investments between stocks and bonds. They try to achieve a return of 7% or greater.
- Income funds provide a dependable steam of income from fixed income or high-paying dividend stocks. They look for a return of 6% or greater.
- Capital preservation funds maintain capital with minimal risk. Their goal is a growth of 5% or greater.

4. An Overview of the Stock Market

Many of us have lived through the rumors of high earnings, high stock prices (bull markets), low earnings, sometimes low stock prices (bear markets), depressions, recessions, crashes, negative returns, positive returns, buy bonds, buy stocks, technology, buy mix of stocks and bonds, bad years, good years, analysts' expectations of growth, whisper numbers, market timing, dollar cost averaging, asset allocations, risk tolerance, time frames and so on.

Since 1926, the average return of corporate profits has run a consistent 7.5% with around 10.9% in returns. Inflation has averaged about 3% for the same time frame.

This section gives you insight into how to assess, calculate, and analyze investments and risk tolerances. You should always understand what you are buying, the tax consequences, and the risk factors before you buy. After all, it is your money.

In 1884, Charles Dow formed The Dow Jones Industrial Average (called the DOW), comprising the top 12 or so stocks that he felt represented the economic strength of America. Since then, the stock market has split into other major components of the DOW:

- Transportation Index
- S&P (Standard and Poor's) 500
- NASDAQ, which was founded in 1971 and consisted mostly of technology stocks
- NASDAQ 100 (known as the QQQ, same ticker symbol), which tracks the top 100 companies
- Russell 2000, which measures small cap stocks (under 500 million in market capitalization)
- Wilshire 5000, which is generally used to measure the total value of all U.S. stocks

- Wilshire 4500, which measures small and mid-cap companies

The U.S. government tracks consumer spending for inflation through the Consumer Price Index (CPI). The Consumer Price Index Urban (CPI-U) represents all consumer spending and accounts for over 80% of all households. Income tax brackets are adjusted based on inflation to prevent higher taxes for consumers. Core CPI is used for longer term inflation trends and tracks food and energy. The Consumer Price Index Wages (CPI-W) adjusts cost-of-living inflation and is primarily used to calculate social security increases (for 2002 the social security increase is 2.6%).

For more information on the stock market and the Consumer Price Index, visit the Bureau of Labor Statistics Web site at <www.bls.gov/cpi/home.htm>.

4.1 Securities Investor Protection Act

The Securities Investor Protection Act of 1970 is the equivalent of bank insurance. The general insurance automatically covers investors for up to $500,000 per customer of the broker or dealer. It is $100,000 for cash.

The U.S. government sponsors this insurance in the form of board appointments made by the U.S. President, the Federal Reserve Board, and the U.S. Treasury. Most brokers or dealers have additional insurance to cover larger losses.

4.2 Investment basics

The following definitions and information should help you navigate the often complicated world and language of investing:

- When you buy or sell a stock, you have a period of time to pay the money due or collect money from the sale. This is referred to as T+3 (trade plus 3 days to settle).

- Distributions are payments a fund makes to investors, from sales of securities held in the fund, interest, and dividends. Distributions are the return (or loss) to shareholders of the fund. Typically, a fund will reissue additional shares rather than make cash distributions.

- When companies pay dividends (generally on a quarterly basis) you can either take the cash or reinvest the dividend into the company stock. The investment company board sets the date that you are entitled to receive the dividend, and you must be a stock recordholder before that date. The

Dividend and ex-dividend: *Dividends are payments declared by the board of directors paid from retained earnings and paid to shareholders of record. Ex-dividend is the time between the announcement of the declared dividend and the payment. The investor who buys shares during the interval is not entitled to the dividend.*

ex-dividend date is generally two business days before the record date to be eligible for the dividend.

- Margin is borrowing against your current portfolio of securities to buy other securities for cash. Generally, you may borrow up to 50% of your portfolio at specified margin interest rates, while your portfolio continues to grow. Many people prefer to borrow — rather than selling their assets.

- Selling short is a sale of a security not owned by the seller. You borrow the security from your broker, and you repay with shares, not cash. It must be a margin account. For example, if you are betting on a decline in the stock price, you would sell short (borrow) at $60 per share. If the market declines, you buy the stock at $40 per share on the open market, which gives you a profit of $20 per share.

- Rule 72 is a rule of thumb to calculate how long it will take your money to double. If your money is earning 6%, divide 6 into 72 = 12 years.

- Mortgage rates are generally tied to 10-year treasury bonds. Adjustable rate mortgages, home equity lines, and credit lines follow the prime rate.

- The federal fund rate is set by the Federal Open Market Committee (FOMC), the federal reserve policy-making division. It is the fluctuating rate that banks charge each other for overnight loans.

- Prime rate is the rate banks charge their best customers. It usually follows the federal fund rate and affects car loans, home equity loans, and corporate credit lines. The rate is controlled by the banks; it is slow to come down, and quick to go up.

- Certificate of deposit rates follow the federal fund rate (see <www.bankrate.com>).

- Bond rates are affected by inflation, interest rates, federal fund rates, and consumer and investor confidence.

- Credit card rates follow the prime rate.

- To calculate your current return on invested capital:
Annual dividend [divided by] current stock price

For example: If your annual dividend is $2.20 and the current price of the stock is $44.375, then 2.20 [divided by] 44.375 = 5% return

- The price to earnings (P/E) helps determine the value of a company. If they are selling at 50 times the earnings, the company may be overvalued. To calculate:
Current stock price [divided by] earnings per share (EPS)

    For example: If the earnings per share are 4.43
    44.375 [divided by] 4.43 = 10 times earnings

- Earnings per share (EPS) are available earnings divided by the number of common stock shares outstanding.

5. Choosing between Commission and Fee-Based Investments

Investments are about choices; understanding what you are buying is important, so is what it costs you. Some investments, such as mutual funds, bonds, and stocks charge commissions, whereas others, such as WRAP accounts, are fee-based.

5.1 Mutual funds

Mutual funds may be either front-end load or no-load funds. Both load and no-load mutual funds have fees that are paid from the pool of money. These include:

- Cost of trades
- Manager fees
- Advertising expenses
- Turnover ratio

The average fund cost runs from 1.6% to 3+%.

Generally, mutual funds are not very tax efficient, and you should ideally look at any overlap and diversification of your funds. (Remember, the top ten holdings may be the same for a value or growth fund.)

You receive an annual step-up in basis for cost each year because you pay taxes at the end of each year on gains. You may

---

Load: *A front-end load fund charges a sales charge or commission upfront to your mutual fund. There is no deferred sales charge, and the fund generally has lower annual expenses. Sales charges vary from 1.6% to 3.5% and up.*

No-load *simply means you do not pay a commission upfront. It has nothing to do with the fund costs you pay for. Fund companies or fund reporting companies such as Morning Star do not report turnover formulas in the cost equation. This could add 1% or more to your total cost of owning the mutual fund.*

Holding: *The stocks, bonds, and mutual funds that are contained in an investment portfolio.*

receive a capital gain distribution even if you lost money in the fund (a tax bill).

5.2 Bonds

When you buy bonds on the open market they contain a mark-up, which can be up to 4%. However, all you see is the price of the bond and the yield. Make sure your bonds have secondary market resale value, as it is generally a lot lower than what you paid.

5.3 Stocks

When purchasing stocks or equities, you pay a commission based on the trade you make with the broker. Depending on the broker, you may pay more than you think. The broker may keep the spread from the bid price and ask price as well as any margin interest they charge.

5.4 WRAP

WRAP accounts are fee-based programs that generally eliminate the confusion of cost. You pay a negotiated fee based on the size of your portfolio, usually an annual fee that is charged quarterly. It takes the conflict out of the trade or recommendation from the broker. The incentive for the broker is to make your portfolio grow — the greater the growth, the greater the income to the firm.

If you buy mutual funds in a WRAP account, you buy Class A shares (with lower expense ratios) at net asset value without all the fund expenses, and you pay the negotiated fee (and any 12-b 1 ongoing advertising trailing fees that run around 0.25 basis points — a basis point is 1/100 of a percent).

If you buy bonds in a WRAP account, you usually buy them at wholesale bid, thus eliminating the middleperson. Your cost is generally lower and your yield higher (bonds can be marked up to 4 points or more, plus you pay for secondary market insurance).

If you buy stocks in a WRAP account, there are no commissions paid in or out.

If you buy, sell, or trade any of these items, generally there are no additional trading or commission costs incurred.

---

margin notes:

WRAP *accounts can be money managers, mutual fund programs, or financial advisor (stock broker) directed.*

Expense ratio: *The charge you pay for your total investment. Includes management fees, operating expenses, trading costs, and sales charges.*

5.5 Discretionary account management

Discretionary money managers (portfolio managers) generally have full discretion to make trades on behalf of the selected risk associated program for an individual or corporate investor.

If you use discretionary account management (i.e., money managers) for your investments, they generally rebalance your portfolio on an annual basis (check, though, whether they do this). They can also provide for better tax efficiency and at the end of the year, and provide you with options if you need to sell off any losses to offset any capital gains from your investments or real estate.

Fees can run from 0.60% to 3% depending on the amount of money invested. Advisory fees are tax deductible on Schedule A if you itemize deductions.

The bottom line, regardless whether you invest in money managers, mutual funds, bonds, or commission programs, is —

- know what your costs are,
- know your investment style and risk category, and
- keep the interest of all parties where they should be — on you and better performance.

6. Stock Options

More and more companies are offering stock options to attract employees. These can be an area of great confusion to many people because of the many rules and timetables of options.

An option is the right to buy or sell property that is granted in exchange for an agreed-upon sum. If the right is not exercised after a specified period of time, the option expires and the buyer forfeits the money. The buyer of a put option is betting the stock will decline in value.

Puts are options to sell stock to the writer or seller of the option that obligate the writer to buy. If the stock declines in value, investors can exercise the right to buy the stock from the writer at the lower market value, and exercise their right to sell it to the writer of the option at the higher agreed-to strike price.

Stock option: *The right to buy or sell property that is granted in exchange for a specified sum. Exercising your option simply means you are buying the agreed exercise price and now own the underlying stock.*

Call option buyers are betting the stock will increase in value. Calls are options to buy stock from the writer or seller of the option and obligate the writer to sell the stock at the lower strike price and sell the stock in the open market at the higher market value.

The seller (or writer) accepts the contract from the buyer at an agreed-to strike (selling) price. The options are on demand, and generally have time limits on them — usually no more than 80 days. The writer hopes the option will expire without exercise, and that he or she will keep the premium paid by the buyer.

To find the break-even point of an option contract, add the strike price to the premium. This is for the buyer and the seller.

The writer is looking for additional income or to balance out his or her portfolio. The buyer is looking to hedge bets against the market without owning the underlying security (the stock). The writer is limited to the premium paid for the amount of profit, while the buyer has the potential to receive higher rewards if the stock performs.

Example 1

> Joe Investor buys a put option on XYZ company for a premium of $300 (the underlying stock is at $40). If the stock drops to $25 per share on the open market and Joe exercises the option (i.e., buys at $25) and then sells the option back to the writer of the put for $40, the profit would be $15 per share. This equals $1,500 minus the $300 premium, or $1,200. If the stock increased or stayed the same, Joe would lose the $300 premium paid and the writer would profit the premium.

Example 2

> Sandra Savings buys a call option on XYZ company for $400. (To buy 100 shares of XYZ stock at $50 per share would cost $5,000. Option contracts are 100 shares per contract). The price rises to $70 during their six-month option contract. Sandra exercises the option to buy the stock from the writer for $50 per share, and sells the stock for $70 on the open market. Her profit is $2,000 minus the $400 premium paid for the option, which equals $1,600 profit for a $400 investment. If the stock does not increase in value or stays the same, the risk is limited to the $400 premium paid for the option.

The Options Clearing Corporation (OCC) issues all options. They are listed on the Chicago Board of Options Exchange

(CBOE). The standard option contract is for 100 shares. All option contracts expire at 3:30 p.m. Central Standard Time on the third Friday of the expiry month. All options have sequential cycles:

- January, April, July, October
- February, May, August, November
- March, June, September, December

Option transactions are reported on Schedule D on your tax return. They do not reflect the holding time frame or the underlying stock for capital gains treatment. The holding period begins on the exercise date of the option. The seller's or writer's holding period ends on the exercise notice.

Option contracts have risk associated with them, and they are not intended for the average investor. There are many types of options, puts, calls, straddles, leaps, index options, covered calls, covered puts, naked options, combinations.

Keep in mind a couple of key elements you need to ask when issued a stock option:

- What is the expiration date (generally 10 years from date of the grant)?
- What is the vesting schedule?
- What does it cost to exercise the options? For example, if you had 1,000 options @ $10 exercise price, it would cost you $10,000 to exercise the options to own the stock.

Vesting schedule: *Companies generally do not want employees to have the ability to sell their stock all at once (employees may leave because they no longer have the incentive to stay). So the companies place time frames on when employees can exercise the options.*

To understand the bargain element (i.e., the taxable portion for basis purposes), use this formula:

	Current market price (the stock)	$80
minus	exercise price (the option)	$20 cost to buy the option per share (=$60 cost basis)
times	the strike price (selling price)	$80 per share
times	the number of shares	100 shares = $8,000-$2,000 =$6,000 taxable portion
equals	the bargain element	$6,000 bargain element times capital gain rate (20% long-term if more than one year, 28% if less than one year).

Understanding Your Investments 95

The cost basis is securities not sold at the time of exercise. It is taxed as long-term capital gain or loss.

The next sections cover the most common types of stock options:

- Incentive stock options (ISOs)
- Non-qualified stock options (NQSOs) or non-statutory stock options (NSSOs)
- Net unrealized appreciation (NUA)

6.1 Incentive stock options

One of the requirements of an incentive stock option (ISO) is that the employee exercise price cannot be less than the stock's market value at the time the option is granted. When the option is exercised, the excess of market value over the excise price goes untaxed. When the ISO shares are sold, the entire profit can qualify for favorable long-term capital gain treatment, provided the sale is more than two years after the option grant date and more than 12 months after the shares were purchased. If the employee sells the ISO shares within two years of the grant or one year of the exercise, it is considered a disqualifying disposition.

Visit the following Web sites to learn more about stock options: www.amex.com, www.fairmark.com, www.networthstrategies.com, and www.888options.com.

A disqualifying position for an ISO results in loss of favorable tax treatment if the sale of the shares bought with ISOs occurs:

- prior to two years from the date of the option grant, or
- one year from the date the shares were transferred to the employee on exercise.

If a disqualifying disposition occurs, the option holder has ordinary income on the date of the disposition (sale) which will be the difference between the fair market value of the shares on the date of exercise and the exercise price.

You can obtain IRS Table 14-1 Worksheet from <www.irs.gov>. Search under "AMT" or "14-1".

The difference between the fair market value and the exercise price counts as positive adjustment for alternative minimum tax (AMT), thus increasing the AMT income in the year of exercise. This may cause the AMT to exceed the employee's regular federal income tax bill. If the employee owes AMT in the year of exercise, he or she may be entitled to an AMT credit to be applied to next year's federal tax return. Use IRS Table 14-1 Worksheet to calculate the AMT, if AMT applies, then transfer the information to Form 6251. Use Form 8801 in the following year to determine if an AMT credit has been earned.

Any gain up to the amount of the difference between market value and exercise price on the exercise date is considered compensation income in the year of the sale. Any additional profit is considered capital gain. The gain is determined by how long the shares (not the options) were owned. If the sales price of the ISO shares is less than the value of the stock on the exercise date, the owner may not have the funds to pay the tax bill under AMT rules. For example, if the stock sold for $20 and the exercise was $80, your tax bill is on $80. If the employee wants to buy back company stock shares after selling ISO shares in a disqualifying position, he or she should wait 31 days to avoid the wash sale rule.

Note: From 2003, the difference between the exercise price and fair market value on the date of exercise on ISOs will be subject to federal employment taxes and federal income tax withholding.

ISOs qualify for charitable gifting and deductions under the Internal Revenue Code. A corporation's charitable deduction in any taxable year may not exceed 10% of its taxable income. A pledged option is a future promise to provide or borrow against a security (in the case, an option). It entitles a corporation to a charitable deduction for the excess of the fair market value on the date of exercise over the exercise price.

If you use derivatives (puts/calls) (see below) on your ISO options, the holding periods are frozen. They reset at zero until the put or call is exercised or expires. To finance your exercise, you can:

- pay cash for the options,
- borrow against securities, or
- sell other securities.

Check with your tax advisor to see if alternative minimum tax or net unrealized appreciation apply (see below).

6.2 Non-qualified stock options or non-statutory stock options

Non-qualified stock options (NSOs or NQSOs) and non-statutory stock options (NSSOs) are can be issued to employees or non-employees (i.e., outside directors or consultants). They can exercise

See Chapter 4 for more information on alternative minimum tax (AMT).

Wash sale rules:
A wash occurs when a bond or stock is sold at a loss and the investor purchases another bond or stock that is substantially identical within 61 days (30 days prior and 30 days after the sale). A wash applies only to losses and is governed by certain rules. IRS recognizes all gains. See IRS Publication 550.

the option at any time and pay ordinary income tax or may hold onto the option for two years after it is issued (granted) for long-term capital gain treatment.

IRS Section 83 does not ascertain a fair market value or recognize income on the date of the grant. Unlike with an ISO, the issuer of a non-qualified stock option has complete flexibility of price. The difference between the exercise price of the NQSO and the fair market value of the stock is taxed as ordinary income at the time of exercise. You must pay in addition to the exercise price when the option is sold —

- federal income tax,
- social security tax,
- Medicare withholding, and
- (possibly) state income tax.

Grant: *A grant is the issue of a stock option. Each option has a grant-registered number assigned with it. A grant allows an investor to exercise the option from a particular date — usually 10 years.*

The cost basis of the stock is the fair market value at the time of exercise. If the stock is sold, it goes down. If it is sold for less than the market price of the exercise date, it is a capital loss.

The employer generally withholds all the taxes at the time of exercise and it shows on your W-2 earnings.

6.3 Net unrealized appreciation

Net unrealized appreciation (NUA) is a lump sum distribution of employer stock or bonds from a qualified plan for which you may elect to pay income tax on the cost basis instead of appreciated value. The difference between cost and market value at the time of distribution is not taxed until the stock is sold. It is taxed as long-term capital gains regardless of when the stock is actually sold, including if it becomes part of your estate. The stock basis will be adjusted by appreciation after distribution from your estate, but the NUA will not change.

For example, if you had 5,000 shares of stock at a cost of $20 per share, the cost of the stock would be $100,000. If the stock appreciated to $80 per share, the market value would be $400,000. The cost ($100,000) is taxed as ordinary income on distribution, while the balance after a one-year hold ($300,000) is taxed as a long-term capital gain when it is sold.

You can also elect to split assets from your 401K. For example, you could elect 2,500 shares of the lowest cost basis shares for distribution and roll the rest along with the balance of assets into a rollover IRA to avoid a taxable distribution. It must be a lump sum in kind distribution based on separation of service, death, or disability.

If you are under 59½ years, the 10% penalty is based on the cost (i.e., the $100,000 in the example above). Make sure you ask what your separation clause reads for transferring assets out of your 401K or defined contribution plan.

Note: You need to keep your statements for the Internal Revenue Service to show your cost basis.

7. Mutual Funds

Many people invest in mutual funds, either for college planning, 401K programs, or individual investing. Mutual funds allow investors to pool their resources as shareholders in a fund, and receive the investment advice of professional money managers. All shareholders share in the dividends, income, and gains (less expenses and fees) of the funds they invest in.

Mandatory distributions are required by the IRS from all qualified retirement plans starting at age 70½.

Mutual funds allow an economical way for modest investors to obtain the same professional advice and diversification of investments as wealthy investors. You may pay $10 per share for a fund, and own several large corporations that you otherwise may not individually be able to afford to buy.

The number of mutual funds available today is staggering; there are over 15,000 funds available in the United States alone. While this variety allows for diversification, it makes it difficult and risky to the average investor to choose the best funds for his or her portfolio. You should seek an advisor to help you establish your risk tolerance, time frames, and objectives to meet the type of funds that may be appropriate for you, as well as to help with diversification.

The Securities and Exchange Commission (SEC) regulates mutual funds. One of the regulations is that mutual funds must be sold with a prospectus to each shareholder. The prospectus explains fees, investment objectives, and expenses, and outlines commissions.

Prospectus: *The official document describing a mutual fund. It must accompany any sales offering to a client within a reasonable time period before purchase of the shares.*

Investment objective: *All funds must have an investment objective (i.e., income, growth, balanced). It must state its objective in the prospectus.*

The operation of a mutual fund consists of:
- Board of directors/trustees
- Officers
- Attorneys
- Independent public accountant
- Custodian
- Administrator
- Transfer agent
- Principal underwriter
- Investment advisor
- You, the shareholder

Almost all funds are all externally managed. They generally have no employees, and hire outside investment managers, broker-dealers, and banks to manage the fund.

7.1 Types of funds

Mutual funds may fall into the following classes:

- Class A shares have an upfront commission or load ranging from 3.5% to 8%. They usually have lower annual expenses.

- Class B shares are no-load upfront, but have declining sales charges (back-end load) over a period of years from the date of purchase (usually six years) ranging from 6% and declining each year.

- Class C shares are generally no-load upfront, but typically have a declining sales charge if taken out before you have owned the fund for at least one year. The charge is usually 1% of the purchase price, and there is usually no charge after one year. They have the highest expense ratio.

- Institution funds, Class D and I are typically sold in defined-contribution or WRAP programs because of the lower expense ratio.

- Exchange traded funds (ETFs) started on the American Stock Exchange in 1993. They are traded like stocks on the open

100   Plan Ahead: Protect Your Estate and Investments

market, generally carry lower commission loads, and can be bought on margin or sold short. There are no capital gains as they are exchanged or transferred, not sold. To find out more, visit <www.amex.com/indexshare_shares_over.stm> or call 1-800-THE-AMEX.

- Index funds imitate the performance of a stock index, like the S&P 500.

Margin is borrowing against your current portfolio of securities to buy other securities or for cash. Generally, you may borrow up to 50% of your portfolio at specified margin interest rates, while your portfolio continues to grow. Many people prefer to borrow rather than selling their assets.

Selling short is a sale of a security not owned by the seller. You borrow the security from your broker. It must be a margin account, and you repay with shares, not cash. For example, if you are betting on a decline in the stock price, you would sell short (borrow) at $60 per share. If the market declines, you buy the stock at $40 per share on the open market, which gives you a profit of $20 per share.

7.2 What tax is payable on mutual funds?

Most mutual funds are open-ended funds. This means that the fund continually issues more shares, and they can be purchased or redeemed (just like stocks) at any time for current value.

Open-ended funds pay a capital gain at the end of each year, which is passed on to each shareholder. Most people do not redeem the gain, but re-invest it back into more shares of the fund at the net asset value (NAV). For example, if you paid $20 per share and it posted a $5 per share gain, the new NAV you purchased additional shares for is $15. The fund share value could lose money, still post a profit, but pass on the loss to you as a shareholder (so you lost value and money and paid taxes).

When you receive your Form 1099B for capital gains, if you re-invested your gains, you pay the tax on that gain, but receive no cash (because you purchased more shares). You hope the value increases over the course of the year, and that you increase your share value as well as appreciation. Each year, mutual funds take a step-up in basis for redemption because you pay your tax each year on any gains.

CDSC charges: Back-end load typically with Class B shares. The deferred sales charge can be as high as 6% over a declining scale of typically six years.

Defined-contribution plan (401K, 403(b)): An employee-funded retirement plan, sometimes matched by the employer.

Closed-end fund: A closed-end fund is one that issues a limited number of shares that trade like a stock. Share prices rise and fall with demand and can sell for more or less than its net asset value.

Open-ended fund: A fund that continually issues more shares, and they can be purchased or redeemed (just like stocks) at any time for current value.

Net asset value (NAV): *The closing price of each trading day reached by taking its total value, subtracting expenses and diving by the total number of shares outstanding.*

Redemption fee: *A charge that may be applied to liquidation of shares held for a short period of time. B or C shares typically carry redemption fees.*

Qualified annuities as IRAs are restricted by the annual limitations allowed by the IRS for contributions per calendar year (in 2002, the limit was $3,000 for an IRA). Non-qualified annuities allow unlimited contributions any time.

7.3 Variable annuities

Variable annuities are a contract issued by an insurance company for retirement planning that allows tax-deferred growth on investments, guaranteed death benefits, and potential income for life.

They may offer some relief from capital gains because they grow tax deferred regardless of whether or not they are a qualified or non-qualified plan. Mutual funds that are available with a variable annuity are called bleeder funds. A company buys the right to use funds from the fund company and micro-manages the funds inside the annuity they sell.

Qualified plans are attractive for mutual funds because of tax-deferred growth.

7.4 Capital gains

Capital gains is a gain on the sale of any property (real estate, stocks, bonds, and mutual funds) less cost basis. Capital gains tax plays an important role in your investment strategy.

- If you are in the 15% tax bracket, you will pay 15% capital gains rate.
- If you are in any other tax bracket, you will pay 20% capital gains after one year.
- If you hold the asset for less than one year, it is a short-term capital gain, and will be taxed at your ordinary rate.

For example, say you buy 100 shares of IBM stock at $80 per share. You sell the stock for $100 per share. Your gain would be $20 per share. If you held the shares for longer than one year, you would pay capital gains tax of 20% of your gain (i.e., 100 shares x $20 = $2,000 x 20% = $400). If you sell your shares before one year is up, you pay ordinary income tax. For example, if you are in the 39.6% bracket, ordinary income tax on capital gains is 39.6%. This is a strong incentive to consider longer term holdings.

Note: The new Temporary Tax Relief Bill allows for a new phase-in of lower tax rates, starting in 2001 and dropping to 35% by 2006. See Chapter 4 for information.

In January 2001, the capital gains rate was lowered to 8% and 18% for assets held longer than five years. The 18% applies only to investments and investors in the higher tax bracket (see income tax tables for new tax law changes) starting in 2001, so to qualify for the 18% tax, you would need to hold your assets until 2006.

You can, however, make a one-time irrevocable decision on assets you already own. This is called a deemed-sale-and-purchase election. It gives the asset a "bought and sold" on a single day, and then qualifies for the 18% capital gains rate. The potential catch is that capital gains could have to be paid the next year on the difference between the original price and the single-day purchase price unless the asset loses value. It takes some serious thought to commit to holding an asset for 5 years. Is it worth the 2% to pay taxes upfront to get there?

7.5 Undistributed long-term gains from closed-end funds

Some closed-end funds elect to pay tax on the gains they realize at their own corporate tax rate and re-invest the proceeds back into the fund rather than distribute long-term capital gains to clients. You must file a separate Form 2439, Notice to Shareholder of Undistributed Long-Term Capital Gains. This is reported on line 64, page 2, of Form 1040. Copy B of the Form 2439 must be attached to your return. Cost basis is increased by the difference between long-term capital gain not distributed and the taxes paid by the fund.

Take care to examine any overlap of investment objectives in the funds you own. For example, your allocation of a growth and income fund may have the same top holdings of a value fund, so your investment balance may not be as great or diversified as you think it is.

You can check out the cost of most mutual funds on Web sites such as <www.andrewtobias.com> or <www.morningstar.com>. Consult a professional tax advisor or financial advisor before making any decision.

8. Bonds

Bonds represent the indebtedness (liability) of their issuers in return for a specified sum (principal). All debt has a maturity date; the date may be from one day to 30 years. Short-term debt generally matures in under a year, intermediate debt usually matures in between one and ten years, and long-term debt is generally ten years or more.

Bondholders receive a fixed interest rate called the coupon rate. The interest rate is usually for the lifetime of the bond duration. The rate of return for the interest is calculated in one of two ways:

- Current yield, which is the annual flow of interest or income, or
- Yield to maturity, which is the yield if the bond is held to maturity and redeemed at par value.

Each debt agreement has obligations that must be met, including:

- date of maturity,
- coupon rate, and
- pledges of collateral.

These are stated in the legal documents.

There are two types of bonds:

- Bearer or coupon bonds, which are bonds that anybody can cash since there are no names on the bonds to identify ownership.
- Registered bonds, which are issued in certificate form in the owner's name. These are held in street name (i.e., the broker holds the security on behalf of the client) if a brokerage account.

All bonds carry ratings established by Moody's and Standard and Poor's. The ratings reflect the ability of the bond's issuer to make all payments in full and on time. Moody's ratings are (from best to worst) Aa3, A1, A2, Ba2; Standard & Poors' ratings are (from best to worst) AA+, A, BBB+.

Bonds carry a risk of default, price fluctuations (i.e., if interest rates rise, bond prices fall; if interest rates fall, bond prices rise), and risk of inflation (i.e., the interest received does not keep up with inflation). Most bonds have a call feature that allows the holder to redeem the bond before maturity. If you paid a premium (1,010) for the bond and it is called before maturity, you receive par (1,000) for the bond. Generally premium bonds offer higher coupon rates, and you can write off the premium on your tax return (amortized over the life of the bond).

For tax purposes, investors may deduct the premium paid at the time of sale of the bond by adjusting the cost basis or by taking an annual deduction for the portion amortized each year. The amortization

Par bonds: *A bond purchased at par value will not have any capital gains due at maturity. If the bond is sold prior to maturity, any change in its value is taxable as a capital gain or loss as with any other investment. If a bond is called, the call premium (if any) is taxable as a capital gain.*

104 Plan Ahead: Protect Your Estate and Investments

of the premium on a bond priced above par is not considered a capital loss. There would be a gain (or loss) if the bond were sold prior to maturity at a price above or below its amortized value.

8.1 Calculating bond yields

Calculate the yield on a bond by dividing the amount of interest it will pay over the course of a year by the current price of the bond. You need to look at yield versus coupon rate as a bond can trade above or below par (face value). The higher the price, the lower the yield. For example,

Check out <www.investinginbonds.com> for more information on bonds.

$$\frac{\text{Annual interest}}{\text{Current market price}} \quad \frac{\$70}{\$1{,}000} = \text{Current yield} \quad (7.0\%)$$

8.2 Bond swaps

Bond swaps occur when one bond is sold and the proceeds are used to buy another bond. An investor may sell a low-coupon bond at a loss for tax purposes and buy a similar discount bond with the proceeds. You establish a capital loss on one to offset the capital gains in other transactions.

Coupon rate: *The interest paid by the issuer of the bond. It may be paid in monthly, quarterly, semi-annual, or annual payments.*

A tax loss swap is the simultaneous sale of one bond and the purchase of a second bond to offset liability from any short- or long-term capital gains. Up to $3,000 of losses against ordinary income can be deducted in any year, and carried forward indefinitely.

You must also abide by the wash sale rules. A wash occurs when a bond is sold at a loss and the investor purchases another bond that is substantially identical within 61 days (30 days prior and 30 days after the sale). A wash applies only to losses. Always check with your tax advisor on wash sale rules as if you break them, you could lose the tax loss and must apply any reportable gains.

You need to look at yield to maturity and yield to call. If the yield is too low, maybe you should find a better investment.

8.3 Taxable versus tax-free bonds

The following will help determine if tax-free bonds or taxable bonds best fit your needs for calculating returns. You can determine what the equivalent rate would be if you bought a tax-free municipal bond as opposed to a taxable bond.

To calculate taxable yields:

$$\frac{\text{Taxable equivalent Yield}}{} = \frac{\text{Tax-exempt yield}}{100\% - \text{tax bracket}}$$

For example, if your tax-exempt yield is 4% and you're in the 31% tax bracket:

$$\frac{4\% \text{ Tax-exempt yield}}{100\% - 31\%} = \frac{4}{69\%} = .0579\% \ (5.58)$$

Table 16 shows the taxable equivalent yields for 2002. If you take the tax-exempt yield of 4% below and are in the 31% tax bracket, you would need a 5.8% taxable security to equal the 4% tax-exempt bond.

Table 16: Taxable equivalent yield (2002)*

CUSIP: *Committee on Uniform Securities Identification Procedures.*

Tax-free yield								
	3.50%	4.0%	4.50%	5.00%	5.50%	6.00%	6.50%	7.00%

Taxable equivalent								
Federal income tax bracket								
15%	4.12%	4.71%	5.29%	5.88%	6.47%	7.06%	7.64%	8.24%
28%	4.86%	5.56%	6.25%	6.94%	7.64%	8.33%	9.03%	9.72%
31%	5.07%	5.80%	6.52%	7.25%	7.97%	8.70%	9.42%	10.14%
36%	5.47%	6.25%	7.03%	7.81%	8.59%	9.38%	10.16%	10.94%
39.60%	5.79%	6.62%	7.45%	8.28%	9.11%	9.93%	10.76%	11.59%

*The new tax laws go into effect starting in 2002 for the new lower federal income tax brackets. The maximum income tax bracket by 2006 will be 35%.

Use Worksheet 11 to decide whether to buy, sell, or swap a bond. It will also help you determine whether you need tax losses or a better coupon rate than you currently have (i.e., a 4% coupon exchanged for a 5% coupon).

Worksheet 11: Tax-loss and swap

Par value	Description	Coupon	Maturity	CUSIP #	Cost basis
_____	_____	_____	_____	_____	_____
_____	_____	_____	_____	_____	_____

Settlement date (i.e., when the bond settles for payment of sale or purchase)
_____/_____/_____

Swap summary:	Sell side	Buy side	Net change
Par value	_____	_____	_____
Annual income	_____	_____	_____
Average coupon	_____	_____	_____
Average maturity	_____	_____	_____
Average price	_____	_____	_____
Average yield	_____	_____	_____
Principal proceeds	_____	_____	
Total tax loss or gain	_____		

8.4 Municipal bonds

A municipal bond is the debt obligation of a state or local government. The funds from the bond may support governmental needs or special projects. A number of different types of municipal bonds exist:

- General obligation municipal bonds are bonds whose principal and interest payments are secured by the full faith, credit, and taxing power of the issuing state or local government

- Revenue bonds are backed directly by the revenues of a particular project, such as a road or bridge.

- Insured municipal bonds are bonds that offer a high degree of credit safety. If the issuer of the insured bonds defaults, an insurance company agrees to pay both the principal and interest when they come due.

- Pre-refunded municipal bonds are good for security. Most of them are secured by U.S. government guaranteed securities.

- Alternative minimum tax municipal bonds are bonds whose interest is subject to the AMT. Some AMT bonds offer high tax-free yields to investors who do not have to pay AMT tax.

- Zero-coupon municipal bonds do not pay interest semi-annually, but are sold at deep discounts to their face value at maturity. You collect all the interest and principal at maturity.

- Original issue discount (OID) bonds that are purchased at an original issue discount give the original purchaser a tax-free capital gain if held to maturity. Selling before maturity at a profit gives the owner tax-free profit for the period held (accreting) — the proportional increase in value that was sold at a discount to face value.

For example, say you buy a 10-year original issue discount bond for $900 (the bond par is $1,000). The bond is held for 5 years and sold at $960. The $60 profit is taxed by the following illustration:

$100 discount [divided by] 10 years = $10 accreted interest

Profit	$60
$10 per year x 5 years held	-$50
Capital gain on sale	$10

If the bond was sold below $950 ($900 plus $50 accreted interest), it would be a deductible loss.

OID bonds require the owner to include as ordinary income each year a pro-rated portion of the discount earned (accreted), for the period held. You must file IRS Form 1099-OID, which indicates the amount to include in income. This adjusts the cost basis each year so you are not taxed twice.

8.5 U.S. treasury bonds

U.S. treasury bonds offer the highest degree of creditworthiness. Timely payments of interest and principal are guaranteed by the full faith of the federal government. Treasury bonds have locked-in interest rates, and the interest is exempt from state and local taxes.

Many municipal bonds contain call provisions that allow issuers to call them prior to maturity. When bonds are called after interest rates drop, investors lose the higher rate of return, and must reinvest at the lower rate. Most treasury bonds cannot be called or redeemed before their final maturity date. Treasury bonds are attractive to the secondary market (i.e., the resale market which establishes the cost basis) because of their no-call fixed-income features and their liquidity.

These are some types of treasury bonds:

- *Treasury notes:* Intermediate-term bonds that are issued in one- to 10-year maturity periods. Issued in denominations of $1,000 to $100,000.

- *Treasury bonds:* Long-term bonds that mature in 10 years or more, issued in denominations of $1,000 to $1 million.

- *Treasury bills:* Bonds that are sold at discount through treasury auctions. The bond goes to the highest bidder. They mature on 3 to 12 months and are issued in denominations of $1,000 to $1 million.

- *TIPS (Treasury inflation indexed securities):* The bonds are indexed with CPI (consumer price index). The interest stays the same; however, the bond value increases to the inflation rate of the CPI. You can receive more value, but cannot receive less than par (1,000).

- *Collateralized mortgage obligations (CMOs):* Bonds that are backed by the broad diversification of several mortgage pools, which reduces risk of prepayment by homeowners. The maturity and yield are difficult to calculate. The underlying pools are backed by a government agency and guarantee timeliness of payments and principal only. They receive the same ratings as other bonds or Government National Mortgage Association (GNMAs) of higher quality and are issued in denominations of $1,000.

- *Series EE bonds:* Appreciation bonds issued on a discount basis (50% of face value). They start at $50 face value. They pay no interest, but increase in value until maturity. You can redeem them prior to maturity. You can either declare an

Understanding Your Investments 109

annual increase in the value of the bond as ordinary income each year or defer taxes until redemption.

- *Series HH bonds:* Ten-year bonds issued in exchange for Series E or EE bonds in denominations of $500, $1,000, $5,000, or $10,000. They are issued and redeemed at par and pay semi-annual interest over the 10-year period. They are subject to federal income tax but do not pay state or local tax.

- *Series I bonds:* Bond that pay two rates of interest: one rate that changes with the rate of inflation and one rate that is fixed. They are sold at face value (i.e., $100 bond will cost you $100), earn interest through maturity (30 years), and pay federal tax but not state or local income tax.

- *Serial bonds:* Bonds that are issued by a corporation to finance a specific use. Equipment is pledged as collateral.

- *Convertible bonds:* Bonds offering a conversion to common stock of the company (generally with lower interest rates). They carry longer maturity dates and are generally callable. If the bond is called, the owner must convert the bond to stock. For example, if the bond was $1,000 and the conversion is for $20 per share you would receive 50 shares of common stock ($1,000 divided by $20 per share = 50 shares).

- *Convertible preferred stock:* Usually used in takeovers of corporations. The Internal Revenue Service has determined that since this would be an exchange in securities rather than a sale, there is no capital gains tax due. So the winning company generally issues or tenders convertible preferred stock with attractive yields to entice stockholders to exchange their shares.

- *Corporate bonds:* Callable bonds issued by companies. If the company issues more stock, it could dilute the ownership of existing shareholders. So instead of borrowing from the bank, the company borrows from the public. Bonds are senior to common stock for security of ownership.

9. Planning for College

The average annual per-person cost for education in private schools in the 1999–2000 tax years was around $22,000, and the average for public schools ran over $10,000. With the rising costs for education, planning for college has become an important part of many parents' investment strategy.

Three commonly used investment strategies for college funding are:

- *Education IRAs:* If you have an educational IRA, you are entitled to save up to $2,000 (See Chapter 4) per year, depending on your income.
- *Uniform Gift to Minors Act (UGM)(UTMA) accounts:* These accounts are limited to the annual gift exclusion and are taxable at the child's rate. By law, the money goes to the child at the age of majority, whether or not he or she goes to college.
- *Educational trusts:* These use the annual gift exclusion for contributions, can run for longer periods of time (as determined by the parent or guardian), and can be used for almost any purpose for the welfare of the child (i.e., to buy a house, for car payments, education). Educational trusts can be complicated to set up, so it is best to consult with an attorney familiar with using them.

9.1 Section 529 college funding

A little-known funding tool was developed under the Federal Tax Act of 1997: Internal Revenue Code Section 529. It is a unique college funding tool that allows anyone to make contributions to almost any college or university. The contributions grow tax deferred for education and higher education. States that establish Section 529 plans are eligible for tax breaks with very few federal restrictions.

The Section 529 plan has a lifetime contribution maximum for each participant — each state has established the maximum amount of contribution education established by the IRS. See Table 17 for the current state limits and visit <www.savingforcollege.com> for more information.

UGMA: The Uniform Gift to Minors Act was established to provide the transference of property to a minor without the use of trusts and using the annual exclusion of $11,000. Gifts can be made by lifetime gift or by will/trust. At the attained age, the child receives the money.

UTMA: The Uniform Transfer to Minors Act allows the transference beyond cash and securities, including real estate, royalties, and patents. The minor cannot take control until age 21 (in some states age 25).

Table 17: Section 529 state current contribution maximums

Check with your state or financial advisor for any changes that may have occurred since this list was published. It is intended as a guideline and for information only.

Arizona	$168,000
Arkansas	$120,000
California	$158,146
Colorado	$150,000
Connecticut	$100,000
Delaware	$120,349
Illinois	$160,000
Indiana	$114,458
Iowa	$140,221
Kansas	$127,000
Maine	$145,000
Massachusetts	$164,375
Missouri	$100,000
Montana	$168,000
New Hampshire	$109,825
New Mexico	$160,539
New Jersey	$246,000
New York	$100,000
Ohio	$158,000
Oklahoma	$100,000
Rhode Island	$246,000
Tennessee	$100,000
Utah	$ 94,600
Virginia	$100,000
Wisconsin	$135,800
Wyoming	$120,000

You can start the program with as little as $250 and make a lump sum contribution of up to $55,000 for each child or individual for a five-year period. Anyone can participate or donate to a Section 529 plan for a specific person. There are no age or income restrictions. For example, Dad could donate $55,000, Mom $55,000, Grandpa $55,000, Grandma $55,000, and Uncle $55,000 up to the total maximum contribution for the plan allowed by your state of election.

The uniqueness of the program does not stop there. The donor remains in control of the money and can withdraw funds at any time. You may also elect a new beneficiary (i.e., another child or a grandchild) to continue the program for higher education. When all beneficiaries are exhausted, you can elect to withdraw the funds (penalties of 10% may apply, as well as ordinary income tax).

Each state offers two basic options:

- *Prepaid tuition plans:* You buy credits and the college guarantees the investment will grow at the rate of college inflation.
- *Managed investment funds:* These are outside investment vehicles.

9.2 Converting to a Section 529 plan

Generally, it is best to establish the Section 529 plan for new contributions to take advantage of the ability to change beneficiaries and maintain control.

UGMA/UTMA accounts allow you to transfer existing accounts into a Section 529 plan. However, to do this, you need to sell your investment and take the tax loss or gain before moving the amounts into the plan. If you transfer a UGMA/UTMA to a Section 529 plan, it carries forward the same restrictions as the UGMA/UTMA account — the IRS rules that once a gift is made to a minor, it is irrevocable (unlike the Section 529 plan, which allows the change of beneficiaries). The transference of the UGMA/UTMA into the Section 529 plan will still grow tax deferred and allow tax-free distributions if used for higher education.

If you are planning to invest for college funding, the Section 529 plan is worth looking into:

- It gives you control of your funds. You can withdraw at anytime, although a 10% penalty may apply, and it is taxed as ordinary income, not as long-term capital gains.
- It allows larger contributions than other plans currently available.

- It removes taxable dollars from your estate (up to a certain percentage).
- It grows tax deferred until withdrawn (if used for higher education it allows tax-free withdrawals).
- You can name or change a beneficiary (even yourself) at the time of establishment, or at a later date to continue the tax-free status if used for higher education.

Note: With the signing of the Tax Relief Act, Section 529 plans now allow tax-deferred growth and tax-free withdrawals. This is in effect until January 1, 2011, when the sunset rule goes into effect, at which time the Section 529 will still grow tax deferred, but will potentially be taxable upon distribution. (See Chapter 4 for more information on the sunset rule.)

You can obtain Section 529 plans directly from participating states. Some states allow tax credits for state-sponsored plans. Check with your financial advisor on other investment options, current tax law changes, and contribution limits.

10. Life Insurance

The main purpose of investing in life insurance is for the death benefit it provides. Life insurance should not be used as a primary retirement benefit. Remember, you need to qualify for life insurance by passing a physical.

Let's look at some facts and purposes for life insurance and how to calculate what you might need. Keep in mind that when an insurance agent calculates your premiums using projected returns (7%, 8%, 9%, etc.), the higher the percentage used, the lower your premium will show. Keep the projections realistic by using percentages ranging between 6% and 7% so you don't have to add money to keep your policy from lapsing. Ask the insurance agent to run the projections to age 100.

Use Table 18 to determine how much life insurance you need. Note, this table assumes that there will be a surviving spouse who will need income.

Table 18: How much life insurance do I need?

Follow this simple formula:

Annual income (surviving spouse):	$_____
Social security benefits:	$_____
Interest/dividends or other income:	$_____
Total income — surviving spouse:	$_____
Annual expenses:	$_____
(Include mortgage, college costs, auto, and food electric; take from budget worksheet)	
Credit card and other debt:	$_____
Final expenses (funeral costs):	$_____
Total expenses:	$_____
Total expenses X life expectancy of surviving spouse:	$_____
Total income minus expenses:	$_____
Liquid assets to pay off debt:	$_____
(Stocks, bonds, mutual funds)	
Life insurance on yourself:	$_____
Total liquid assets: (cash)	$_____
Shortfall:	$_____

Incidence of ownership: *The power to change beneficiaries, borrow against the cash values, surrender the policy, or pay premiums directly.*

10.1 Taxation of life insurance

Life insurance will be income tax free to your beneficiaries if:

- the policy is held in your name or there is an incidence of ownership, or
- the estate is named the beneficiary.

Bear in mind, however, that it will be taxable at the face value of the estate, and the interest earned is also taxable.

The gift value for gift-tax purposes of a life insurance policy is equal to the fair market value of the life insurance policy. If the insured gifts the policy and dies within three years, the proceeds will be included in his or her gross estate for estate tax purposes.

10.2 Loans

Policy loans are generally not treated as taxable distributions, even if the loan exceeds the policy owner's cost basis. A lapse, however, of a contract with an outstanding loan will result in the treatment of the loan, including accrued interest, as a distribution and may be taxable. Loans are deductible from the face value of the policy proceeds at death.

Section 1035 of the Internal Revenue Code allows for tax-free exchange of one life insurance contract for another. As a general rule, the existing law provides that no gain is recognized if the contracts are exchanged as long as the insured parties are the same.

Many different types of life insurance exist. Each type has a specific design depending on your needs at various levels and stages of your life. Let's take a look at some of them.

10.3 Irrevocable life insurance trust

An irrevocable life insurance trust (ILIT) is a separate trust that owns the life insurance policy(s) for the benefit of named beneficiaries. Upon death, the proceeds are income tax free and estate tax free.

You cannot have any incidence of ownership (i.e., write checks directly to the trust for premium payment) or the IRS will bring back the policy into the taxable estate. An ILIT is generally funded using crummy trust powers (see Chapter 5, Trusts, for more information).

Existing policies carry a three-year look-back provision for estate tax purposes. After three years, they are estate tax free. New polices are estate tax free with no look-back provisions. The IRS can go back three years under will, or five years under trusts.

10.4 Term policies

A term policy is a policy that you pay into for a specific term (e.g., 10, 15, 20, or 30 years). They are attractive to single people as they

---

Irrevocable life insurance trust (ILIT): *A trust established to own life insurance polices and remove them from your taxable estate and provide tax-free and estate tax-free dollars to your beneficiaries.*

Crummy power: *The power held by the beneficiary to withdraw a certain amount of money annually from the trust.*

are generally inexpensive (depending on age and health) and they guarantee your insurability at a later date. Most term polices have a conversion clause that allows you to change your term policy for whole or variable life (see below) at a specific scheduled date in your policy.

Decreasing term policies are popular for insuring a mortgage. These policies decline with the balance of your mortgage. Some parents choose to buy their children a term policy that has a conversion clause at a later date for them. Again, this ensures insurability.

10.5 Traditional whole life policies

Traditional whole life policies combine a death benefit with an accumulation of cash benefit (cash value). The cash benefit is a preset amount of interest applied to your fixed premium for the life of the contract.

10.6 Universal life policies

A universal life policy is a variation of the traditional whole life policy. It allows you to adjust your premium payments and death benefit up or down as your need or financial position changes. You can use cash values to pay the premium.

Be careful however, if you allow cash values to pay for the policy and it runs out of money, because your policy could lapse. You can choose to pay more into the policy to increase the cash value. The investments are interest credited by the insurance company to your policy.

10.7 Variable universal life policies

Also called flexible premium adjustable variable life. This policy is designed to give policyholders flexibility for premium payments, death benefits, and investment objectives. The money is held in and invested into a separate account, which contains investment choices of various mutual funds (growth, balanced, bonds, etc).

If you do well on the investments, your cash value or death benefit increases. One way to keep up with inflation is to use an increasing death benefit (i.e., return of account value). Remember, the policyholder bears the investment risk in this type of policy.

10.8 Wealth replacement trust

This is another name for a life insurance policy, and is generally used in a charitable remainder trust (see Chapter 5, Trusts). The most common policy is a second-to-die policy. When the second spouse dies, the money in the trust goes to charity and the life insurance policy goes to the beneficiary income tax and estate tax free.

The policy is placed in an ILIT, which removes incidence of ownership to keep it non-taxable for federal estate taxes. Life insurance is taxable at the face value of the policy for federal estate tax purposes if the policy is in the owner's name. In most policies, you don't want to accumulate cash values (return of account values), because you generally do not receive both death benefit and cash value. Apply the cash value accumulations to the premium to offset costs.

10.9 Single premium life policies

With a single premium life policy you buy a fixed amount of death benefit for your beneficiaries, and usually place it in an ILIT. This removes it from your estate (remember, life insurance is taxable on the face value of the policy if left in your name). The single premium policy replaces lost income from charitable trusts, pays for any additional estate taxes due, provides income or cash for surviving beneficiaries, and, if inside the trust, is income and estate tax free. Since it is a single premium, once you pay for it there are no more premiums to worry about.

10.10 Key person policies

Key person policies are used to replace a "key" person that may be running a company in the event of his or her death. The company can use the funds to have cash to hire and replace that individual.

Key person policies are important for business owners. They help them decide on their future by giving them enough cash to have the option of running the business, buying out existing partners, or hiring a new person to run the company. If you run a business, it makes sense to look into business succession planning. Buy/Sell agreements are used for selling a business between associates or owners.

10.11 Long-term care policies

Long-term care insurance provides nursing home care, in-home care, or assisted living care. You must qualify for this insurance by passing a physical. Unfortunately, most people wait until they are older to apply for long-term care insurance, when they are less likely to pass a physical.

Be careful in selecting coverage. The length of benefit means that if you buy a four-year benefit, at the end of four years your benefit expires and you are on your own. Daily benefits are what the maximum amount per day is for 365 days. If you have $150 per day benefit (i.e., $54,750) and your nursing home costs are $70,000, you must pay the difference.

Check whether the policy pays 100% or 80% toward medical care and prescriptions. Most carriers provide spousal discounts and compound or simple interest for inflation. Ask your advisor to show you an illustration to see if the benefit increase is worth the extra premiums. So far, long-term care premiums have been stable, but as the baby boomers start using more benefits, the premiums are likely to increase. See Chapter 7, Looking after Your Health, for more information.

10.12 Disability policies

Disability policies are designed to replace your income at a certain percentage — generally 60% or 40% of your wages — should you become disabled and unable to work. Short-term and long-term policies are available. Select coverage that best meets that need and your budget. It's a good idea to have a nest egg of three to six months to pay for expenses to help meet eligibility waiting periods.

10.13 As a retirement investment

Some of the advantages of using life insurance as a retirement investment are tax deferred growth, death benefits, availability of low-cost loans, and cash value withdrawals — generally all without tax consequences. You do have the cost of insurance and premiums to pay, usually for the life of the policyholder or until endowment.

Beware, though, if you fund the policy for retirement and the policy has accumulated a large amount of cash due to good investment growth. If you start taking out annual withdrawals for retirement and the policy lapses because of failure to make premium payments from the loans, you could be facing a tax bill on the investment gain you made on your portfolio. The tax bill would be:

Loans − premiums paid = portfolio gain X your tax bracket.

Ouch, that could really leave a mark!

11. Variable Annuities

An annuity is a contract issued by an insurance company that guarantees the investor will not run out of money through equal annual sums. As with mutual funds, bonds, and life insurance, investors can choose from a wide range of investments. Let's examine some of the reasons for buying annuities.

Annuities: *Often annualized step up death benefits of 5% or more, or portfolio value (whichever is greater, less any distributions).*

11.1 Investors

Annuities are popular with the following investors:

- Investors who buy mutual funds but don't want or need the current taxable income and choose to reinvest their earnings on a tax-deferred basis.

- High-income investors who have maximized their retirement plans. Annuities allow unlimited (non-qualified only) contributions and grow tax deferred. They also eliminate the 70½ rule for mandatory distribution, avoid probate, and can provide income for life. Rollover 401K/IRAs carry the same rules in annuities as the IRA 70½ rule applies.

11.2 Family protection and estate planning

Annuities have changed over the years. Some offer annualized step-up with guaranteed death benefits, multiple investment managers, guaranteed principal, tax-free transfers, and income streams or lump sum distributions. Annuities avoid probate and other final expenses, and do not require you to pass a physical.

Using annuities for A/B credit shelter trusts is an excellent tool for investment because of their tax-deferred position. Trusts pay taxes at the highest rate very quickly, and in tax-deferred vehicles no income is generated by the trust, so no taxes are paid until distribution.

Assets placed inside the trust grow estate tax-free forever. See Chapter 5, Trusts, for more information.

11.3 Qualified plans

Annuities may be suitable for transfers of existing qualified plan assets and new contributions. This includes 403(b), IRA, SEP, and Simple IRA lump sum distributions and partial transfers.

Annuities may also benefit 403(b) participants who generally have poor choices and very little support outside of a toll-free telephone number to call. Under the IRS 90/24 Rule (In-service Distribution), you can transfer the vested portion of your 403(b) to another qualified 403(b) vehicle such as a variable annuity (which often has better features, such as the step-up guaranteed death benefits, and better investment choices). You would maintain your payroll deduction to the plan, and roll out vested parts of it on an annual basis.

Pension plans that use cash or allow cash transfers are very attractive. Under most pension rules, when the pension spouse dies, the pension amount is generally reduced by up to 60% for the surviving spouse. The pensions are generally reduced again when Social Security kicks in. If the money is transferred to an annuity, the surviving spouse has two options:

- Receive income as the surviving spouse and new contract owner with no reduction in income (possible increase if the separate accounts have performed well)
- Lump sum distribution

Most variable annuities offer a step-up in death benefits on an annual basis, avoid probate, and generally the income stream continues with no additional tax consequences to the surviving spouse.

403(b): A non-profit defined contribution plan (410K is a for profit).

11.4 Current annuity owners

Investors who own fixed or older annuities and seek higher returns or the additional benefits of newer products, can complete tax-free transfers under the 1035 exchange rule. Make sure you check on back-end charges and other expenses before you make the exchange. Also check to see if your guaranteed death benefit is higher than the portfolio value before you make the exchange.

11.5 Guaranteed income (annuitization)

Annuities are attractive for people seeking security against living longer than their money lasts. Annuities provide a guarantee in the form of a contract (annuitized contracts) between the insurance company and you, and are backed by the strength and ability of the insurance company. Look for A.M. Best A+ ratings.

11.6 Charitable giving

A charitable remainder trust can invest in variable annuities, which maintain its tax-deferred status instead of being taxed at trust rates. Variable annuities provide an income stream and current tax deduction for the donors with survivorship rights.

Generally a wealth replacement trust is established (life insurance policy) to provide income and federal estate tax–free money for the heirs or beneficiaries, and a lump sum distribution to the charity upon the death of both donors. It also provides a guaranteed death benefit to the charity.

11.7 Fixed charitable gift annuity

A fixed charitable gift annuity provides an amount of fixed income for both donors at a set rate of return and a current tax deduction. This is similar to buying bonds for more secure investments.

11.8 Medicaid planning

Planning for Medicaid takes professional knowledge, and you should consult with a professional consultant, planner, or attorney before making this type of investment. Be prepared for your medical requirements by purchasing long-term care policies and life insurance, or setting up trusts.

Each state has different laws about allowable income for the community spouse (the one not in the nursing home). The common investment is a single premium immediate pay annuity. The community spouse may be entitled to unlimited income, and the asset is removed from the countable asset list for Medicaid. These are usually irrevocable transfers of assets. See Chapter 7 for more information about Medicaid planning.

11.9 Don't annuities cost too much?

According to Lipper Analytical Services, based on 1997 data, the cost difference between variable annuities and mutual funds is only about 0.65%. Mutual funds generally have a higher management fee (1.38% versus 0.81% for variable annuities). The higher overall cost for annuities is due to the special insurance services provided, tax deferral, guaranteed death benefits, and lifetime income option.

Most annuities have declining sales charges over a period of generally seven or eight years. Each year the charge decreases until it disappears. The declining sales charges are not applied if there is a systematic withdrawal for retirement purposes. Check the prospectus and compare total fees and services of annuities against mutual funds to make sure you are making the best investment for your needs. Refer to Table 19 for a comparison of mutual funds and annuities.

Remember that annuities are designed for long-term investment strategies. A 10% penalty may apply from IRS if you withdraw money from a variable annuity before the age of 59½. See the rulings outlined below for IRS rule of 72t for early withdrawal from any qualified plan to avoid the 10% penalty.

11.10 What happens when the owner of the annuity dies?

The Internal Revenue Code requires that a deferred annuity contract be distributed to the designated beneficiary within five years of the death of the contract owner. However, if the contract owner's designated beneficiary is the surviving spouse, the contract may be continued with the surviving spouse as the new owner. If the contract owner is a trust, the death of the annuitant is treated as the death of the owner.

If the owner dies prior to taking distributions, the distributions must be done within five years of the owner's death. Unless it is a surviving spouse, he or she can take new ownership of the contract without creating a taxable event as long as the new owner begins payments within one year of the owner's death. If it is a non-spouse beneficiary, he or she can take distributions over his or her life expectancy as long as payments begin not more than one year after the owner's death.

The annuity death benefit of a non-qualified variable annuity is the gain of all appreciation above corpus (original contribution) and is taxed at ordinary income. An exception is a variable annuity purchased before October 20, 1979. All contributions made prior to that date get a step-up in basis at death. The benefit becomes income tax-free to the beneficiary.

11.11 How are annuities taxed?

The Tax Equity and Fiscal Responsibility Act of 1982 (TEFRA) changed how deferred annuity contracts are taxed. Before August 14, 1982, any withdrawal from an annuity was taxed as a return of basis first. After the entire basis had been withdrawn, the gain would be taxed. This is referred to as the first-in, first-out (FIFO) method of taxation. For contracts issued on or after August 14, 1982, withdrawals are taxed first on gain, with return of basis last, also known as the last-in, first-out (LIFO) method of taxation. Contracts with pre-TEFRA premiums that are tax free may be exempt from the new rules. Any subsequent payments would be considered post-TEFRA premiums.

All qualified and non-qualified annuity contracts have the same tax treatment for early withdrawals. A 10% penalty is imposed on any withdrawals made before reaching age 59½. To avoid the 10% penalty, you may elect the IRS Sec. 72 (t), which allows distributions to be made in substantially equal periodic payments for the greater of five years or until the attained age of 59½.

IRS Notice 89-25 provides three safe harbor methods for taxation of substantially equal periodic payments:

- *Amortization method:* Instalment payments are computed by spreading the account balance over a number of years to equal the life expectancy of the account holder or the joint life expectancy of the account holder and the beneficiary. A reasonable rate of interest is included in the calculations. The computed amount remains constant for the duration of taking equal periodic payments.

- *Annuitization method:* Payments are computed using an annuity factor (the present value of a straight life annuity of $1 per year beginning at the account holder's age in the first distribution year) with a reasonable rate of interest included in the annuity factor. This remains constant for the periodic payment.

- *Life expectancy:* Payments are calculated by spreading the account balance over a number of years equal to the life expectancy of the account holder (and/or account holder and beneficiary). The distribution amount must be recomputed each year under this method using the prior year-end balance and the life expectancy factor based on the attained age (or ages).

Annuity owners receive Form 1099-R from the insurance company by January 31st following the year in which a taxable distribution has been made.

11.12 Indefinite deferral of income

IRS rules prevent indefinite deferral of income through successive ownership on the gain in an annuity. These are not or should not be used for estate planning to pass on to children and grandchildren. Better vehicles would be a Roth IRA or irrevocable life insurance trust. The IRC states that:

> The gain portion of a non-qualified variable annuity is subject to both income tax and federal estate tax because the property of the decedent had a right to receive income during his or her life, and would have been included in gross income if so received. To offset the double taxation, a deduction is allowed on the beneficiary's income tax return for the amount of estate tax paid of the gross amount of the gain that was taxable in the gross estate. The amount of the deduction is determined by comparing the actual estate tax paid to a hypothetical estate calculation made without including the gain in the annuity.

For a short illustration of the above: Your taxable income from an annuity of $300,000 would be $141,000 ($300,000 less prepaid IRD tax of 53%, i.e., $159,000). Multiply that by your tax bracket of 36%, and your income tax payable would be $50,700 — which makes an effective tax rate of 17%.

11.13 Gift or sale of an annuity

Prior to April 23, 1987, if a gift or sale of an annuity contract was given to another person at a time when the cash surrender value exceeds the donor's cost basis, there was no taxable event at the time of the gift. However, at the subsequent surrender of the contract, the donor had to pay tax (and report) on any gain that existed at the time of the gift when it was surrendered.

After April 23, 1987, if the gift or sale was given at the time the cash surrender value exceeds the donor's cost basis, the donor must include in his or her taxable income the gain for the year that the transfer took place. The rule does not apply to transfers between spouses.

IRD tax: *Tax paid on income in receipt of a decedent.*

The person who sells an annuity or surrenders the contract must report any profit in the year as ordinary income. If the annuity contract was sold for less than he or she paid for the contract, there is a deductible ordinary loss.

11.14 Annuitization of an annuity

Payments of the annuity stop on the death of the owner and are not included in the federal gross estate. Payments received are treated as ordinary income. Unless they were received during the payout period of a certain option, any unused portion of the period will be brought back into the estate for estate tax purposes.

Lump sum distributions are taxed at ordinary income on the gain in the annuity, and will receive the same IRD tax credit for federal estate taxes paid.

The payments received during lifetime of the annuitant (owner) are a blend of principal and gain in the annuity taxed at your current income tax bracket.

Annuities are not FDIC insured, and could lose value, including your principal. Always check with a professional, read the prospectus, and evaluate the risk of annuities (or any investment) before purchasing. Know what the costs are for transferring or liquidating an annuity (e.g., CDSC charges or deferred sales charges).

12. Mutual Funds versus Annuities

There are advantages to owning both annuities and mutual funds. Both, along with other investments, can help make a balanced investment and retirement strategy. Make sure you read the prospectus and compare the products before making any investments. Check with your financial advisor, tax advisor, or other professional prior to making any decisions.

Table 19: Comparison of mutual funds and annuities

	Variable annuity	Mutual funds
IRD taxation advantage	yes	no
Tax deferrals	yes	no
Guaranteed lifetime incomes	yes	no
Guaranteed death benefits	yes	no
Tax-free transfers to other annuities	yes	no
1035 exchange transfers among funds with no tax consequences	yes	no
Bypass probate	yes	no
Professional asset management	yes	yes
Tax treatment allows investor to select investment based on potential return, not tax efficiency	yes	no
Unlimited contributions (non-qualified)	yes	yes
Deferred sales charges	yes	most/no
Guaranteed principal		yes
Capital gains tax every year (even if you do not make a profit or gain)	no	yes

Use Worksheet 12 to keep track of your investments.

Understanding Your Investments 127

Worksheet 12: Keep Track of Your Investments

Type/ Investment	Date/ of Purchase	# Shares/	Purchase/ Price	Symbol/ CUSIP #	Market Value /	Broker/Bank	Account #
						Phone #	On-line access code
						Date Sold	Capital Gain/Loss

Mutual Funds

_____ _____ _____ _____ _____ _____ _____ _____
_____ _____ _____ _____ _____ _____ _____ _____
_____ _____ _____ _____ _____ _____ _____ _____

Stocks

_____ _____ _____ _____ _____ _____ _____ _____
_____ _____ _____ _____ _____ _____ _____ _____

Bonds

_____ _____ _____ _____ _____ _____ _____ _____
_____ _____ _____ _____ _____ _____ _____ _____

Stock Options
Option / Date of grant / expiration / # options / vesting dates / NSO/ISO / exercise date / exercise price / # shares sold / profit / Grant #   of option

List each option separately.
Personal Residence: Date of Purchase _____ Purchase Price $ _____
500,000 exemption on capital gains on sale of primary residence every two years for joint, 250,000 for single. Anything above exclusion is subject to capital gains tax

Notes:

128   Plan Ahead: Protect Your Estate and Investments

7
LOOKING AFTER YOUR HEALTH

In Chapter 6, we discussed the need to plan for retirement. The age for collecting Social Security is increasing, while the benefits are decreasing. One in five people over 50 (and 43% of people over 65) will require some form of nursing home care. More women will require nursing home care than will men.

Under the Health Insurance Portability Act of 1996, the federal government has made it clear as to who is responsible for nursing home care — you! Do you have enough insurance to cover your medical needs as well as your living expenses? Know the rules, because the stakes are high.

This chapter discusses some of the options available to you, including Medicaid, Medicare, and long-term health care policies. Remember, you have a choice when planning for your future health. Make a good one based on an understanding of your assets, your family health history, and knowledge of what you are buying.

1. What Is the Difference between Medicare and Medicaid?

Medicaid is a joint federal-state health insurance program administered by the state.

Medicare is a federal health insurance program administered by the Centers for Medicare and Medicaid Services. Medicare covers only 20 days of nursing home care at 100% and requires that the nursing home stay be immediately following a hospital confinement.

To receive Medicare, you must have made 40 quarters (i.e., 10 years) of payments to FICA and FUTA. If you have paid fewer than 30 quarters of covered Medicare employment, you qualify for Medicare for a premium of $319.00 per month. If you have paid for 30 to 39 quarters of covered employment, the premium is $175.00 per month.

Regular Health Maintenance Organization (HMO) or Health Insurance does not cover nursing home care, and very few Medicare supplemental policies cover nursing home care. The national average cost of a nursing home is over $40,000.

Resources:

Medicaid: <www.hcfa.gov>

Medicare: <www.ssa.gov> or call **1-800-633-4227**

Nursing Home Comparisons: <www.medicare.gov/nhcompare/home.asp>

2. Medicaid

Medicaid is a joint federal-state health insurance program administered by the state. Each state has different rulings on income testing and countable assets. When you apply to Medicaid for assistance, they will calculate your estate at that moment and will use this evaluation for any declaration on ineligibility or to figure look-back violations.

If you are over the asset limits or have violated the look-back provisions by gifting away assets, Medicaid will declare you ineligible for a period of time equivalent to the violation.

As well, the Medicaid recovery rules allow Medicaid to become the first creditor in probate court. This means that when you die, any amounts owing to Medicaid are paid first (out of your home, personal assets, and personal property) before your heirs receive their share.

2.1 Countable assets

Nearly all assets that may be placed on a net worth statement are considered countable assets for the purposes of Medicaid. These include all bank accounts, certificates of deposit, stocks, bonds, mutual funds, life insurance, annuities, and residences, except where there is a surviving spouse.

Non-countable assets are assets that are beyond the reach of Medicaid, such as a Medicaid qualified trust, your personal residence (if the surviving spouse is not in nursing home), one family car, your personal jewelry, and a burial policy.

Check your state's requirements for countable assets. For example, New Jersey allows a community spouse's pension plan and qualified savings such as IRAs or 401Ks to be included as available resources for Medicaid eligibility.

2.2 Spend-down of assets

This is sometimes called "involuntary poverty" or "forced poverty." Prospective Medicaid patients are required to spend away all their personal wealth to a maximum limit of around $2,000 (each state's limit varies). If you exceed the limit by $1, you could become ineligible for Medicaid.

Under the rule of the halves, however, each state allows the well spouse to divide the family assets in half and allow the spend-down only to the portion of the person requiring Medicaid. This limit is generally around $74,000 to carry the second spouse for the remainder of his or her lifetime. If the second spouse requires nursing home care, the remaining half of the estate will also be lost.

2.3 Look-back provisions

Look-back provisions enable you to move assets out of your name into your beneficiary's name. After the look-back is complete, Medicaid has no claim on the assets. The look-back provisions are:

- 36 months for regular transfers
- 60 months for a trust

A word of caution: Exchanges or gifting of more than $11,000 per person or $22,000 joint could trigger a gift tax violation (see Chapter 4 for more information). An outright sale of assets is best as it avoids all claims. To qualify for the purposes of the IRS and Medicaid, the sale must be based on fair market value (i.e., an asset sold for no less than 70% of its value, as determined by an independent appraiser).

2.4 Fair market exchanges

A way of avoiding the look-back and spend-down provisions is to sell your residence or property for fair market value (70% or more

Look-back provisions: *The amount of time the IRS allows for a transfer of an asset out of the taxable estate. The transfer may not exceed the annual exclusion for gift tax purposes. The largest collector for Medicaid and the IRS is probate.*

of its value) and buy a single premium immediate annuity (SPIA). These are trusts that convey the assets into trust by a fair market purchase using an exchange of trust certificates. Talk to your financial advisor about your options.

3. Long-Term Health Care Policies

As we discussed in Chapter 6, social security and pension plans often provide insufficient funds for retirement, especially if you need to pay for expensive health care. Table 20 shows the social security benefits that have been available over the last few years. Consider whether these amounts will be enough for your retirement.

Table 20: Social security benefits

Social Security/Medicare	2003	2002	2001	2000	1999
Cost of Living Increase	1.4%	2.6%	3.5%	2.4%	1.3%
Social Security Wage base	87,000	84,900	$80,400	$76,200	$72,600
Medicare Wage Base	unlimited	unlimited	unlimited	unlimited	unlimited
Social Security Tax Rate*	6.20%	6.20%	6.20%	6.20%	6.20%
Medicare Tax Rate	1.45%	1.45%	1.45%	1.45%	1.45%
Medicare: Part A (hospital) deductible**	$840	$812	$792	$776	$768
Medicare: Part B (medical services) premium***	$58.70	$54	$50.00	$45.50	$45.50
Maximum Social Security Benefit	$1,741	$1,660	$1,536	$1,433	$1,373

*15.30% for self-employed

** Less deductible per benefit period. For the first 60 days, deductible is $840. For the next 30 days, deductible is $210 per day. For the next 60 days, the deductible is $420 per day for each lifetime reserve day (total of 60 lifetime reserve days non-renewable) benefit period. Skilled Nursing: First 20 days: no charge, next 80 days patient pays $105 per day, after 100 days patient pays 100%.

***Part B: $58.70 per month with a $100 deductible per year.

One of the best ways to protect your assets from Medicaid is to buy a long-term health care policy. If you are thinking about doing this, don't wait until you are older. You must qualify with a physical, and your health is less desirable to an insurance company when you are older. As well, the cost of a long-term policy will probably be less over a longer term.

Most long-term health policies allow you to design your own plan, daily dollar benefit, and elimination periods around your budget.

Use the following checklist when looking for your policy:

- ❑ Does the policy provide for in-home care, a nursing home, or assisted care living? Most people would rather have proper health care at home. Some policies will also pay for assisted living facilities.

- ❑ What is the premium? Remember, premiums are not guaranteed. Although they have been stable over the years, they could go up at some point in the future.

- ❑ Is there a waiver of premiums if you are confined to a nursing home, assisted living, or in-home care for any length of time? Do the premiums continue if you are released?

- ❑ Does the policy plan for simple, compound, or no inflation? If you are purchasing a policy while still young, compounding may make more sense, but as you get older, simple or no inflation may be more beneficial. Find out what your state costs are for an average nursing home and divide that by 365 days. This will give you your daily benefit needed. Also, find out what inflation or increases have occurred over the last five years in nursing home care. This will help you determine what inflation factor you need to put in your policy. You can choose a compound policy now and at a later date lower it to a simple or no inflation policy. However, you cannot increase your coverage without re-establishing a new policy.

- ❑ What is the benefit period of the policy (i.e., the length of time that the benefits will cover)? This is often the most confusing part of the policy. Remember, if your benefit is for four years, at the end of four years your benefit is gone. Always ask for quotes on an unlimited benefit as well.

- ❑ Does the policy cover amounts up to 100% or 80%? Does it cover prescriptions?

- ❑ Is the policy portable (i.e., if you move to another state, is the policy valid for that state)? What is the actual aggregate time of coverage?

Elimination period: The period of time that you pay the nursing home or in-home care before your policy takes over.

☐ Is the policy tax deductible? New laws have made some long-term health care policies tax deductible (see below). Check with your accountant to find out if you qualify.

☐ Does the policy offer spousal discounts? (Most do.)

☐ Are Alzheimer's, senility, Parkinson's, and dementia covered?

3.1 Tax deductions

Make sure the company underwriting the long-term health care policy is reputable with solid finances.

If you bought a long-term care policy before January 1, 1997, you are allowed to make a deduction on your taxes for long-term care insurance as a medical expense, subject to the 7.5% floor. The benefits may not be treated as income. Most people will not meet the medical deduction because of the 7.5% floor. After January 1, 1997, you must have purchased a tax-qualified policy to take advantage of the medical deduction. It is still subject to the 7.5% floor.

The 7.5% floor means that any premiums you pay that are more than 7.5% of your income are eligible for deductions off your income tax.

A non-tax-qualified policy includes a benefit trigger referred to as "medical necessity." This allows your doctor to determine if medical necessity will override the normal qualifiers for the policy. Some medical necessities may include:

- Inability to carry out activities of daily living, such as bathing, dressing, eating, or toileting.

- Functional impairment, such as Alzheimer's, senility, or dementia.

If you have a qualified plan, the tax deductions you receive are:

If you establish a special needs trust for an individual, your state of domicile Medicaid division will probably want to review the trust or will before approval and funding of the trust.

Age	Deduction
40 and under	$ 200
41– 50	$ 375
51– 60	$ 750
61– 70	$2,000
70 +	$2,500

The deductions will increase annually, adjusted for the medical care component of the consumer price index. Check with your insurance company or financial consultant for more details on new policies, qualified policies, and any tax law changes.

GLOSSARY

1099: Untaxed income from any source. It could include income from dividends, capital gains, or self-employment where no tax is withheld (i.e., commissioned salespeople).

403(b): A non-profit defined contribution plan (410K is a for profit).

A/B Trust: Marital trust, by-pass trust, a trust to place your unified credit exemption. The A trust is for living spouse; the B trust is for deceased spouse.

Administrator: Person named to administer the estate by the court.

Adjusted Gross Income (AGI): Income less adjustments.

Alternate Beneficiary: Person who receives assets if primary beneficiary dies.

Alternate Valuation Date: The date is not to exceed six months after the date of death. The value of the assets must be lower and result in a reduction of the gross estate to qualify.

Alternative Minimum Tax (AMT): A tax calculation to ensure individuals and trusts do not escape federal tax liabilities. They need to calculate regular income tax and AMT and pay the highest tax.

Ancillary Administration: Probate of property or assets in another state (unless in trust).

Annual Exclusion: The annual amount in each taxable year you may gift to an individual: $11,000 per individual, 22,000 joint, as of December 31, 2001.

Annuity Trust: An annuity trust pays a fixed annual amount to a beneficiary for the term of the trust agreement.

Asset Allocation: The proper investment mix for an investor. Based on time frames, goals, needs, objectives, and risk tolerances.

Assignment: Transferring your interest in any asset to another party. Used commonly in trusts.

Attained Age: In most states, the attained age is 18 for men and 21 for women.

Basis: What you paid for an asset. Determines taxes for gains and losses.

Beneficiaries: The individuals or corporations that receive assets from the estate after probate or from trust.

Bequest: A specific bequest is a gift by will of a designated class or kind of property.

C Corporation: A legal entity as identified by the IRS that pays dividends, has shareholders, a board of directors, and stock. Unlike an S corporation or limited liability company, the C corporation must pay tax on income and before dividend distribution

CDSC Charges: Back-end load typically with Class B shares. The deferred sales charge can be as high as 6% over a declining scale of typically six years.

Certificate of Trust: Verification of the trust. It explains the powers of the trustee and identifies any successor trustees.

Charitable Gift: Gifts of cash or property to a qualified charity in which the donor receives tax deductions, income, estate and capital gains benefits.

Class A Beneficiary: son, mother, husband; **Class B**: cousin, aunt, nephew.

Closed-Ended Fund: A closed-end fund is one that issues limited number of shares that trade like a stock. Share prices rise and fall with demand and can sell for more or less than their net asset value.

Codicil: An amendment to a will.

Conservator: An individual (guardian) legally responsible for the care of another individual.

Contest: To dispute the terms of a will.

Corporate Trustee: An institution that manages assets for a trust.

Corpus: The principal property of a trust.

Coupon Rate: The interest paid by the issuer of the bond. It may be paid in monthly, quarterly, semi-annual, or annual payments.

Creditor: Individual or corporation that is owed money.

Crummy Power: The placement of the power of appointment into a trust. This allows additions to the trust to qualify for the annual gift exclusion. The trust beneficiaries have the right to withdraw trust assets up to the annual exclusion.

CUSIP: Committee on Uniform Securities Identification Procedures.

Custodian: Individual who manages assets for minors under the UTMA (uniform gift to minors act).

Defined Benefit Plan: A corporate sponsored retirement plan.

Defined Contribution Plan: An employee funded retirement plan, sometimes matched by the employer. [401K, 403(b)].

Disclaimer Provision: The allowance of the beneficiary (generally the surviving spouse) to refuse acceptance of certain assets for federal tax purposes.

Dividend and Ex-Dividend: Dividends are payments declared by the board of directors paid from retained earnings and paid to shareholders of record. Ex-dividend is the time between the announcement of the declared dividend and the payment. The investor who buys shares during the interval is not entitled to the dividend.

Durable Power of Attorney Financial: Allows full or partial authority of an individual to make decisions and transact business on your behalf in the case of incapacity. The appointment can be by will provisions, trust instruments, or appointed by the courts.

Durable Power of Attorney Health Care: Allows full or partial authority of an individual to make decisions for health care in the event you are unable to (incapacity). The appointment can be by will provision, trust instruments, or by the courts.

Dynasty Trust: An irrevocable life insurance trust (ILIT) used by wealthy individuals to create a non-taxable generation skipping transfers for several generations.

Elimination period: The period of time that you pay the nursing home or in-home care before your policy takes over.

Equity: The current net value of an asset.

ESOP Employer Stock Option Plan: A defined contribution plan investing in the employers stock.

Estate: The total value of all assets of an individual(s). Used to determine estate taxes, state death taxes as determined by an independent appraiser for IRS purposes.

Estate Taxes: Federal taxation on the assets in an estate less the unified credits and debts. Federal estate taxes are net; state death taxes are from the gross estate.

Executor: Person or institution named to carry out the instruction set forth in the will or trust instrument.

Executor/Executrix: The person or individual who takes your Will to Probate, collects the assets, orders appraisals, makes payments, and distributes the estate according to your Will. This individual is personally liable for the investments. Any beneficiary has the right to sue him or her for any losses in values. Make sure you make him or her aware of this fact.

Expense Ratio: The charge you pay for your total investment. Includes management fees, operating expenses, trading costs, and sales charges.

Fair Market Value: Items that are sold at 70% or better are considered by the IRS to be sold at fair market value.

Fiduciary: Person or institution who has the legal right to act for another person. Generally in financial matters.

Funding: The process of transferring assets into your trust.

Gain: The difference between what you paid for an asset, and what you sold it for (Capital gain).

Generation Skipping Transfer: Currently a $1.1 million each (indexed for inflation) GST exemption that allows you transfer property or cash for two or more generations for inheritance purposes.

Generation Skipping Transfer Tax: A transfer tax assessed on gifts in excess of $1.1 million to grandchildren, great-grandchildren. The tax is at 55%.

Gift Exclusion: The annual amount allowed per individual to gift to another individual in each calendar year. Currently $11,000 individual, $22,000 joint. Commonly used to fund GST, Legacy trusts, and Life Insurance Trusts (crummy trusts).

Gift Tax: A 55% tax (gradually reducing to 35% by 2009) IRS imposes on any gift exceeding the annual gift exclusion. Penalties can range from 200%–400% plus the current % gift tax.

Grant: A grant is the issue of a stock option. Each option has a grant-registered number assigned with it. A grant allows an investor to exercise the option from a particular date — usually 10 years.

Grantor: A person who creates a trust or directly or indirectly makes a gratuitous transfer of property to a trust (which includes cash). If the person creates or funds a trust on behalf of another person, both persons are treated as grantors of the trust.

Guardian: The person or individual who will take care of your children and make decisions on their behalf until they reach attained age. If no guardian is appointed, it could be the state.

Heir: An individual entitlement by law to receive part or all of an estate.

Holding: The stocks, bonds, and mutual funds that are contained in an investment portfolio.

Incapacity: Describes an individual who is no longer capable of handling their own medical or financial affairs. It may be permanent or temporary. Generally requires court intervention and supervision to protect the individual from wrongdoing.

Incidence of Ownership: Life insurance policies have incidence of ownership. This means that you have the ability to change beneficiaries, and write checks and withdraw cash from a policy. However, if you do any of these things, the IRS will bring the policy back into your estate for tax purposes.

Inheritance: Assets received from the net proceeds from an estate.

Inter Vivos: A trust established while you are alive.

Investment Objective: All funds must have an investment objective (i.e., income, growth, balanced). A fund must state its objective in the prospectus.

IRD Tax: Tax paid on income in receipt of a decedent.

Irrevocable Life Insurance Trust: (ILIT) A trust established to own life insurance polices and remove them from your taxable estate and provide tax-free and estate tax-free dollars to your beneficiaries.

Irrevocable Trust: A trust that cannot be revoked or cancelled.

Intestate: Without a will.

Joint Tenants with Right of Survivorship: (JTWOS) Property that transfers automatically to the surviving spouse, with the assets being taxable in the surviving spouse's estate.

Lifetime Transfer: Each calendar year, you can gift $11,000 without reducing your unified credit or paying the gift tax over the annual exclusion per person. If you live to 90 years, you can do this about 90 times. The lifetime transfer would be approximately $1 million.

Limited Liability Company (LLC): An entity formed under state law by filing articles of organization as a limited liability company. None of the members of the LLC are personally liable for its debt. One of the primary uses for LLCs is to shelter rental properties. If each property has its own LLC, any entity that sues for damages or injury would have to sue each LLC. This means that the liability is limited to that property, not all properties — and not to the individual.

Living Will: A document that states your wishes in reference to artificial means to keep you alive if you have a terminal injury or illness. Also called a health-care proxy

Load: A front-end load fund charges a sales charge or commission upfront to your mutual fund. There is no deferred sales charge, and the fund generally has lower annual expenses. Sales charges vary from 1.6% to 3.5% and up.

No-Load simply means you do not pay a commission upfront. It has nothing to do with the fund costs you pay for. Fund companies or fund reporting companies such as Morning Star do not report turnover formulas in the cost equation. This could add 1% or more to your total cost of owning the mutual fund.

Look-Back Provision: The IRS has the power to bring back a policy into a taxable estate. For existing policies, they can go back three years under a will, or five years under trusts. New policies do not have a look-back provision.

Medicaid: A federal program in which you trade assets for nursing home care.

Medicare: A federal health care program for individuals over 65 who are covered by social security.

Net Asset Value (NAV): The closing price of each trading day reached by taking its total value, subtracting expenses and diving by the total number of shares outstanding.

Non-Marital Tax Exclusion: The non-marital tax exclusion is used when the all assets from your estate are transferred to your surviving spouse. It avoids estate taxes, but is fully taxable in the surviving spouse's estate. It is best to place the non-marital deduction into a B trust, otherwise you will lose that amount of the unified credit.

Open-Ended Fund: A fund that continually issues more shares, and they can be purchased or redeemed (just like stocks) at any time for current value.

Par Bonds: A bond purchased at par value will not have any capital gains due at maturity. If the bond is sold prior to maturity, any change in its value is taxable as a capital gain or loss, as with any other investment. If a bond is called, the call premium (if any) is taxable as a capital gain.

Pour Over Will: A will that states any assets left outside your living trust will become part of your living trust.

Power of Attorney: A legal document giving an individual or corporation power to transact business on your behalf.

Powers of Attorney are used if you or your spouse becomes incapacitated, and you want someone else to make decisions on health care and financial affairs for you. Your will does not cover this; since you are not dead, it becomes court appointed.

Probate: The court process of validating your will, paying debts, and distributing assets according to the wishes of your will.

Prospectus: The official document describing a mutual fund. It must accompany any sales offering to a client within a reasonable time period before purchase of the shares.

Qualified Terminal Interest Property Trust: Assets transfer into the QTIP trust upon the death of the donor and provide income for the surviving spouse. QTIP trusts assure that the remaining assets will transfer to the rightful heirs.

Qualified Personal Residence Trust: The QPRT trust holds the title to the donor's primary (or vacation home) residence and the donor retains the right to live there for a specified period of time. It removes the property from the estate.

Redemption Fee: A charge that may be applied to liquidation of shares held for a short period of time. B or C shares typically carry redemption fees.

Revocable Trust: A trust that allows the donor to change, revoke, or cancel the trust any time. A revocable trust is considered a grantor trust and is taxed to the grantor rather than to the trust.

Rollover Provisions: Individuals can transfer (rollover) previous 401Ks and IRAs from previous employers or consolidate several IRAs into one account. Rolling the account over avoids making it a taxable event. In order to avoid the 20% mandatory withholding, the rollovers should be made out to the broker or bank for the benefit of the individual.

Second-to-Die Policy: A life insurance policy in which nothing happens to the policy when the first spouse dies. When the second spouse dies, the money is distributed according to the wishes of his or her will or trust.

Special Needs Trust: A trust established to take care of an individual who is not capable of doing so himself or herself.

Spendthrift Trust: Protects assets from creditors, and restricts or limits spending by the beneficiary.

Sprinkle Provision: Gives the trustee discretionary authority to distribute income or principal in unequal amounts to beneficiaries.

State Death Taxes: A death tax imposed on estates in addition to federal estate taxes.

Step up in Basis: An asset that has passed through probate or from a trust. The new value is considered the new "basis" moving forward for tax purposes for the heirs. Generally it avoids capital gains and gift taxation after passing through probate or from a trust.

Stock Option: The right to buy or sell property that is granted in exchange for a specified sum. Exercising your option simply means you are buying the agreed exercise price and now own the underlying stock.

Successor Trustee: The individual or institution that takes over, as trustee should the first trustee die, resign, or become incapacitated.

Testamentary Trust: An unfunded trust inside a will. It does not avoid probate and could trigger gift tax and capital gains tax.

Testate: An individual who dies without a will.

Testator: An individual who leaves a will in force at death.

Trustee: An individual or institution that manages and distributes assets for another, or for oneself as in the case of a Revocable Living Trust.

Trustee: The person or individual appointed by the executor to hold the testator's assets should the testator have left minor children. The executor manages the money until the children reach attained age. The successor trustee is someone other than you or your spouse. There is a need for a successor trustee is in the event both husband and wife die. While one or both of you are alive, you are the trustees. Some states hold the trustees liable for any losses in portfolio values; any beneficiary has the right to sue that trustee for the losses. You may consider a corporate trustee for this service.

UGMA: The Uniform Gift to Minors Act was established to provide the transference of property to a minor without the use of trusts and using the annual exclusion of $11,000. Gifts can be made by lifetime gift or by will/trust. At the attained age, the child receives the money.

UTMA: The Uniform Transfer to Minors Act allows the transference beyond cash and securities, including real estate, royalties, and patents. The minor cannot take control until age 21 (in some states age 25).

Unified Credit: The exclusion from federal estate taxes: $675,000 for 2001, $1 million 2002, and increasing to 3.5 million by 2009, back to 1 million in 2011.

Unitrust: A unitrust pays income to a beneficiary as a fixed annual percentage of the trust assets' value. The percentage remains the same for the entire term of the trust agreement.

Vesting Schedule: Companies generally do not want employees to have the ability to sell their stock all at once (employees may leave because they no longer have the incentive to stay). So the companies place time frames on when employees can exercise the options.

Wash Sale Rules: A wash occurs when a bond or stock is sold at a loss and the investor purchases another bond or stock that is substantially identical within 61 days (30 days prior and 30 days after the sale). A wash applies only to losses and is governed by certain rules. IRS recognizes all gains. See IRS Publication 550.

Will: A written legal document administered and distributed through the probate process according to your instructions.

Resources / Web addresses:

Resources	Web addresses:
Internal Revenue Service	www.irs.gov www.irs.gov/govts (this is for federal/state/local web page)
Social Security	www.ssa.gov
ERISA for qualified plans	www.freeerisa.com www.info@erisaconsulting.com
IRA	www.irahelp.com www.pensionplanet.com www.mpowercafe.com
Mutual Fund calculator	www.andrewtobias.com
Mutual Fund information	www.morningstar.com

Bonds	www.investinginbonds.com www.giftlaw.com
Legal	www.findlaw.com
National Association of Securities Dealers	www.nasd.com
Social Security	www.ssa.gov
Medicare (1-800-633-4227)	www.ssa.gov
Medicaid	www.hcfa.gov

List of forms needed for filing income and expenses for a decedent:

These IRS Forms and instructions may be obtained at <www.irs.gov>.

Form 1041: U.S. income tax return for trusts

- Administrative expenses: Form 1041 or Form 706 (Form 706 is filed for unified credit exemption)
- Business income: Final Form 1040, 1041, Schedule C & F (cash and accrual method)
- Business tax credits: Form 1040 and Form 3800
- Capital gains: Form 1040 Schedule D, Form 706 and Form 1041
- Casualty and theft loses: Form 1041 or Form 706 Schedule L
- Charitable contributions: Form 1041 Schedule O
- Claims against decedent's estate: Form 706 Schedule K
- Credit for the Elderly or Disabled: Final Form 1040 Schedule R

You need to contact your attorney and accountant to help in the preparation of filing all appropriate forms, death certificate, Form 706, final 1040 or 1041 for trusts, etc. Bills still must be paid: contact the creditors (you should have a list of all creditors with phone numbers/fax and e-mail addresses) and let them know of the death. Most states have a time frame before you can file for probate; find out what that time frame is.

Find out how to apply for Social Security benefits at <www.ssa.gov>.

WILLS GUIDE FOR AMERICA

Robert C. Waters, Attorney

$16.95

1-55180-283-X

- Save legal fees
- Make your own will

If you die without making a proper, valid will, your family and relatives may become involved in expensive lawsuits or struggle through months of paperwork. Your assets will be distributed according to state law, not according to your wishes.

This book explains why and how you should draw up a will. Examples of the common will forms used in the US are included.

Questions addressed include:

- What are the requirements for a valid, effective will?
- Do you need a lawyer?
- What is an executor?
- What is a community property agreement and how does it work?
- What are the tax advantages of a will?

ORDER FORM

All prices are subject to change without notice. Books are available in book, department, and stationery stores. If you cannot buy the book through a store, please use this order form.

(Please print.)

Name _____

Address _____

Charge to ❑ Visa   ❑ MasterCard

Account number _____

Validation Date _____

Expiry date _____

Signature _____

YES, please send me:

___ Wills Guide for America
    $16.95

Please add $5.50 for postage and handling.

Washington residents, please add 7.8% sales tax.

❑ Check here for a free catalog.

Please send your order to:

Self-Counsel Press Inc.

1704 N. State Street

Bellingham, WA 98225

Visit our Internet Web site at:
www.self-counsel.com